Kassos

When Myth becomes Reality

by

David Leesley

Penwith Press

First published in 2014 by:

Penwith Press
Cornwall
United Kingdom

www.penwithpress.co.uk

ISBN: 978-0-9533316-6-6

Typesetting, design and layout:
Jonathan How
www.coherentvisions.com

Acknowledgements

Catherine and Cliff Bell, Mo Colley,
Elizabeth Kelsall, Jill Moss,
Helen and James Young

Contents

Philippines

Kiribati

Papua New Guinea

Solomon Islands

Indonesia

Vanuatu

Australia

New Zealand

Preface

In the West we believe that divinity is external and above us, which may descend to humans. Christianity rejected the Gods and Goddesses of the Old Way, isolating, disconnecting and abandoning them in a sterile Heaven which was always out of reach. However, most indigenous peoples believe that Deity is below us, rising and manifesting through the earth and Mother Nature to support us, interacting and communicating as our ancestors do with us from within. We are never alone. The Great Cosmic Mother, creator of all life does not need our pathetic little prayers; we need them to fulfil a state of inner grace, peace and hope.

There can be no problem – physical, emotional, mental or spiritual – that cannot be solved once we have discovered our Inner Divine Nature, our True Selves. In essence, we are the bi-product of the psychological and emotional baggage of our parents and their lineage for at least the previous seven generations. Someone has to decide for the pain to stop, to free the individual and the next seven generations to come. Let us be part of the solution, rather than the problem.

We are the sacred children that the Earth Mother has been waiting for to reunite her with the Sky Father. If we become disconnected from the mother, the father cannot work through us to wipe away her tears. When we lose our indigenous tribes, who hold this connection, we, in the West, die a little more each day. We have become a spiritually crippled race.

Around the turn of the 20th century there were estimated to be 30 million species of life on this planet. In 1993 there were estimated to be 15 million species. It took billions of years to create these life forms and, within one hundred years, man has destroyed half of the species. It is estimated that over 200 atomic bombs have been detonated above and below ground, causing catastrophic toxic discharges and shock waves that undoubtedly have caused fracturing in the sensitive geological structures within the earth, which in turn will alter volcanic and earthquake activity and the weather. As a race, we have broken Cosmic Law (see Appendix A). Sadly, the more technically "advanced" we become, the more we lose our connection to Reality and Spirit, falling into illusion.

Our forefathers betrayed the earth and the wisdom keepers of our world for generations through greed, fear and violence. The future is composed of thoughts not yet materialised. We have the choice to create our future or let it be created by our indecision.

It is time for us to act. Let us right these wrongs now. To dispel the darkness our ancestors created, our generation must turn on the lights!

Vanuatu

Torres Islands

Banks Islands

Espiritu Santo

Ambae

Maewo

Pentecost

Valo

Malekula

Ambrym

Paama
Ulveah

Epi

Shepherd Islands

Port Vila ● **Efate**

Erromango

Matthew & Hunter Islands

Aniwa

Futuna

Tanna

Aneityum

Introduction

This book is the sequel to *Return of the White Serpent* (Penwith Press, 2012), which gives the background information to this one. Through a series of synchronicities beginning in 2003, David, the White Serpent, became reunited after many generations with his spiritual twin, the Black Serpent, on a small tropical island, Tanna, in the Republic of Vanuatu, South Pacific. Through secret ceremonies and tribal myth, he learned of a bizarre connection to the Isle of Man (British Isles) where David was born and raised.

This is the story recorded in his journals of his continued spiritual awakening and self-discovery through an ancient culture that is dying and soon to become extinct. High Chief Wai Wai Rawi has given David permission to reveal his tribal secrets to the West for the first time. This story is not meant to be a boring, tedious, intellectual work, rather a story told simply about a vanishing lifestyle which is on the brink of succumbing to the sickness of Western influences and, because of this, the disconnection to the Earth Mother, Sky Father and the ancestors (Spirit).

High Chief Wai Wai Rawi is the last authentic High Chief of his lineage and tribe and still remembers, as a small boy, listening to the old men of his grandfather's generation tell their stories of Majikjiki their God, cannibal feasts and the Kassoso, the Dragon men, around the nakamals, their sacred temples in the forests. Only those of the High Chief lineage are permitted to know the truth. I have earned that privilege.

Anthropologists have now found out, through DNA and other specialised testing, that the Pacific Islanders, including the Australian Aborigines, are the most ancient of the human races, and from which all of the other races have evolved. (The only exceptions are the Hottentots and Bushmen of Africa.)

High Chief Wai Wai Rawi belongs to this ancient lineage, a lineage that understands that everything that exists in the physical world must be created and exist in the non-physical world first... The Realms of the Ancestors.

Tanna Island

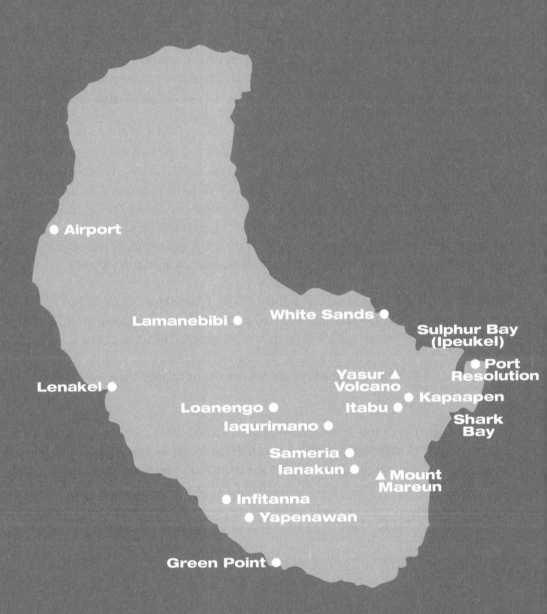

Unable to locate many of the villages visited with any accuracy

Dedication

To Maggie, High Woman Natu Elin

Part 1
The Calling

I n 2008, my wife Maggie went through her initiation with High Chief Wai Wai Rawi to receive her grade mark (tattoo) and her tribal name Natu Elin. We were then married at Itabu village the Chief's home. The name Itabu means "forbidden place".

In September 2010, when Natu and I were in Itabu village, High Chief Wai Wai Rawi asked us to return to the tribal lands in 2013 to attend the principal Tokka Ceremony and Festival, which was held approximately every four years in different parts of Tanna Island, principally the west. The Chief explained that this was the most important festival in the tribal calendar and, as such, we were expected to attend because of our tribal grades. In 2011, I only received two letters in return from High Chief Wai Wai Rawi, which was very frustrating as I had written several to him with the usual list of questions to be clarified and answered. I knew that some of his letters didn't arrive. One of the problems the Chief has is that, due to the high humidity in the summer months especially, any envelope he can obtain loses its adhesive so many letters (envelopes) I received were open and some pages were clearly missing. One of the Chief's letters, which I received in May, told of how the kitchen house of Donald, his firstborn son, had caught fire and burned to the ground and that Donald's wife Namu was expecting another baby. Thankfully, nobody was hurt in the fire.

Maggie's Grading Ceremony, when she received her tribal name in 2008

In November of the same year, I received the High Chief's second letter which explained that the Chief, who was organising and holding the Tokka Festival, had changed the date from 2013, as previously planned, to 2012. The festival was to be held at Imanakulamine. No specific month was given. I wrote again requesting specific dates, if possible, but, like most indigenous peoples, dates are never "set in stone" and festivals and ceremonies are held when the time and local conditions are right, including guidance from the ancestors, whenever that will be. Patience is essential when working with indigenous tribes. The problem for Westerners, of course, is that, because of our regulated, constrained and controlled lifestyles, we have the need to look ahead to take time off work, book flights and other travel arrangements. After spending an obscene amount of hard-earned cash on flights arriving in Vanuata (or elsewhere) for an indigenous ceremony that doesn't take place for whatever reason, it is frustrating to say the least. Tribal peoples live for the moment; they live in the now, not thinking ahead to the future or to the past, as we in the West tend to do. They also live in harmony with the cycles of nature and have all the time in the world. They have little or no understanding of the false and disconnected way that we live our lives in the West, so become surprised and somewhat bemused when we become impatient, frustrated or angry when arrangements agreed upon do not take place.

In early February 2012, news of a devastating cyclone that had battered the southern islands of Vanuatu arrived by an unexpected source. My biological twin brother Barry works as a security officer at the ferry terminal on the Isle of Man and one of his colleagues Anna works in the Manx Tourism Department. Anna coincidentally has a sister, Liz, who lives in Port Vila, the capital of Vanuatu, and runs her own business there. Barry had mentioned to Anna that Maggie and I worked with a tribe on Tanna Island, so Anna relayed this message to her sister, along with my brother's contact details. When Cyclone Jasmine hit Vanuatu, Elizabeth Kelsall contacted Barry directly to see if we were on Tanna at that time or not. She explained that she was the Honorary Correspondent in Vanuatu to the British High Commission in Suva, Fiji, and, as Vanuatu no longer had British diplomatic services, she needed to know the whereabouts of all British nationals to see if they were safe. She asked Barry if I would contact her so that our names could be added to her "Expat List". I emailed Liz who very soon became a valuable contact to relay messages to the High Chief via Michael, the Chief's nephew, who understood and spoke good English. Liz found out through her network of contacts that the Chief and his family were safe but that Port Resolution, not far from Itabu, had received a severe battering. Many crops were destroyed, so the local authorities were waiting for the Red Cross to get food down to that part of the island.

A few days after this contact through Liz, I received a letter from the Chief posted in January asking that Natu and I come for the Tokka Festival for the whole month of September 2012 as there were also other ceremonies to be performed. The Tokka Festival was now going to be held at Yatapu. This caused me great anxiety, since I had been asked to give a presentation about the tribe and to teach a workshop at the British Society of Dowsers (BSD) Annual Conference in England in September. I didn't know what to do as I had given my word to attend the BSD Conference, yet I had a unique opportunity to reconnect to the Kassoso (the Dragon men) as well as attending the Tokka Festival. The Chief wrote in his letter saying, 'My brother, I had a dream. It is true that the spirits have proved to me that you are a guardian of the sacred skulls. The skulls are on an island.' This cryptic message intrigued me. I agreed to honour my BSD commitments, emailing Liz in Port Vila to see if she could relay a message to the Chief to explain that I could not come in September but could I do more ceremonies to connect with Kassoso in August instead. I would miss the Tokka Festival again, unfortunately.

As we waited for a reply from Liz in Vanuatu, Maggie and I worked out our finances and came to the unfortunate conclusion that we couldn't afford for both of us to return to the tribal lands on this occasion. I would have to travel alone. As Maggie and I are both self-employed, we simply could not afford to take a month each off work, plus the travel costs for two. Maggie was very disappointed since she wanted to experience the Tokka Festival as her grade mark tattoo represents the sacred Tokka stick. Since the Chief and I had had the encounters with the Kassoso in 2010, I have been practising with different shamanic techniques and had felt a shift in my vibration. I have made stronger connections to the dragons and the Dragon Riders. I feel ready now; before, I was not sufficiently prepared.

2nd March 2012:
Kassoso wanted to kill me
In a shamanic journey I connected with the Kassoso, going back to the camp in the rain forest where the Chief and I slept in 2010. It was dark, yet I was aware of the Kassoso emerging from a portal and moving through the damp tropical undergrowth. I saw the leaf shelter that the Chief, Donald and I had erected and watched as a shadowy dark figure approached the palm leaf door flap, peering inside. I was surprised at what I saw – there, lying asleep inside the shelter were the Chief and me! I was the observer and the observed. The Dragon Man approached me first for some reason, extending a black, bony, claw-like hand, pulling back the light blanket that covered me. In his other hand, he held a pointed fighting stick. I saw the Dragon Man's eyes glow red in the darkness, then saw three other sets of glowing red eyes behind where I stood, observing myself. I understood the esoteric principle of time being a man-made concept, yet here I was going back in time to

my past where I had travelled back interdimensionally but, interestingly, I was no longer in the past as I was in the "now", observing myself, or a part of myself, in a different time. This was the first time I had experienced journeying shamanically into my immediate past and bilocating, being in two places at the same time but in a conscious way. I also understood that the same principle can be used for moving into my future.

Once I had grasped the wonder and simplicity of this, I watched myself stirring in the shelter. The Dragon Man raised his fighting stick to strike me but the clawed hand of another stopped him. My would-be attacker had a bat-like face, yet the other being who had shown more restraint and compassion had more human features. I recognised the fighting sticks the Kassoso carried; they were larger and longer versions of the sharpened hunting sticks that the men used to throw, boomerang-like, into the flying fox (bats) roosts high in the canopies of the banyan trees. I thought this was a very interesting concept, who developed these fighting sticks first – humans or Kassoso?

Now I was back in present time in the form of a Kassoso myself! The Dragon men were somewhat startled at first and didn't know how to react but we both stood our ground as equals, but from different races, cultures and dimensions. Then they departed swiftly, melting back into the darkness of the forest and through the portal to their own world, wherever that was?

3rd March 2012:
Kassoso Star Gate
Once again through a shamanic journey, I travelled to a secret meeting place in the rain forest and shapeshifted into the form of the Kassoso. This time, the Dragon men were more amenable towards me as I approached them as near as I could in their own form. They had created an interdimensional portal or star gate between two particular trees which I was permitted to visit and experience. In the darkness of the night, the portal looked like a huge oval scrying mirror. What was interesting was that flashes of electricity that looked like pale blue lightning ran around the perimeter of the portal as if this force was somehow holding the interdimensional star gate in place. As I looked up into the clear night sky, I could see countless stars above the tree canopy; yet, when I looked into the portal, all I saw was a dark empty void.

One of the Dragon men moved forward towards me, offering me one end of a sharp pointed fighting stick which he carried in his right hand, indicating through body language and telepathy for me to hold the stick offered to me, but not to take it. I realised that the Dragon Man was going to act as my guide into the black void and I knew I must not let go of the stick under any circumstances. This Dragon Man was going to be my soul shepherd to enable me to have safe passage in a place beyond time that has no beginning or end. The prospect was exciting, yet also somewhat alarming. I had come so far over the years with the Chief guiding me and preparing me for moments like these through sacred ceremony and with my own shamanic journeys. I was now ready; had I not been this possibility could not occur, so I took great comfort in that.

I took hold of the stick as instructed, looking deep into the red burning eyes of my companion. I called upon Majikjiki, the tribal god, and my trusted spirit allies to accompany and protect me as I approached the star gate into the unknown. The lightning activity around the rim of the portal increased dramatically as we stepped into what felt like a cool black cloud, which was much different to the heat and humidity of the jungle we had just left behind. We entered into a place of total darkness, stillness and peace – a place where no form was apparent except for my companion. I recognised this place, as I had been here before, or at least somewhere similar when I had done shamanic journeys into the dark void of the sacred womb of the Earth Mother. Could it be the same place, I wondered?

The same thing happened as before; I began to fall, to spin, to descend into a stream of unknown black energy where I felt and observed my energetic body dissolving until I was formless, only being aware of my connection to the Kassoso's fighting stick and the red glowing eyes beyond its other end. I felt totally at peace within the velvet black fluidity of the sacred womb and the full potential of being birthed into any form within the cosmos. It felt as if I was in the intra-universe, the place between the molecules and atoms of our own world, a place so deep that it is impossible to describe. I had no fear, as I had trusted completely in my companions with me. I was formless, shapeless, I was nothing and no thing, yet I was everything or had the potential to be everything.

At that moment, I received the insight that it was my sacred birthright to reach my full potential by being bigger and brighter. I also realised that by manifesting my True Self my personal boundaries were strengthened, aligned and impregnable. Those who constantly build protective boundaries around themselves simply drain their vitality through fear. I was aware that time did not exist where I was, so we may have been in this "no place" for eons or seconds? I became aware of my energy body coalescing back together magnetically returning and reforming into a crystalline matrix, a new lifeform to rebuild my emerging form.

We passed back through the portal into the rain forest to its welcome familiar sounds and smells. I was instructed to let go of the Kassoso's fighting stick. I turned to thank my companion but he and the others had already passed back through the star gate into the void. I stood alone under the myriad of stars in the night sky watching the foraging flying foxes silhouetted against the full moon and the fireflies playing tag amongst the foliage. I could see everything around me with such amazing clarity, as if I had been reborn into a new world which, in essence, I had been. I felt a deep peace; I felt free.

9th March 2012:
Earthquake

I received word that a major earthquake (measuring 7.1 on the Richter Scale) with severe tsunami warnings had devastated Erromango, the neighbouring island to Tanna where the ancestral skulls are. I went online to get more information from the Vanuata Geohazards Observatory website (VGOW), which monitors volcanoes, earthquakes and tsunamis, and also the Vanuatu Government Meteorological Services website which is issued by the Ministry of Infrastructure and Public Utilities Department. I could find little more than basic information from either source.

10th April 2012:
Travel Problems   Grade Belts

I received an email from Liz in Port Vila to say she had contacted Michael, the Chief's nephew on Tanna who said that, if I were to come to Itabu in August, the ceremonies to connect with Kassoso would still go ahead without problem as they were completely separate from the Tokka Festival. I sent an email to my travel agent requesting approximate costings for flights to Vanuatu for August, receiving a reply a couple of days afterwards which was extremely disappointing as the costs were prohibitive and way above my budget. It transpired that most flights around that time had been prebooked some time previously because of international travel for the London Olympics and Paralympics. The only seats available were limited to business class and first class. August had to be ruled out now.

The only other possibility left to me because of other commitments I had was to go after the BSD Conference at the end of September and arrive in Vanuatu for October. I sent another email to Liz in Vanuatu, asking her to contact Michael again to see if I could come to Itabu in October instead. After a couple of days I received a reply from Liz to say that the Tokka Festival dates had changed yet again to October and it was fine for me to arrive then! The true diplomat that Liz was reminded me that the local people tend to change their minds often so nothing could be guaranteed. I enquired with the travel agent about the possibility of flights for my revised dates and found that there was no problem booking seats. Fortunately, they were £1,000 cheaper at this time. In due course, Maggie booked my return flights from the Isle of Man to Tanna Island giving me a stop-over break in Singapore both ways. I had made the financial commitment now and had saved another £500 by booking online through an Internet travel provider. I felt that my journey back to the tribal lands was beginning at last. It was time to prepare.

In 2005, I undertook a ceremony where the Yeramanu (Shamanic) lineage was conferred upon me and, after that initiation, I was presented with my Grade Belt, the God Belt, made from the bark of the female banyan tree. The sacred mark upon the belt was the Serpent. This bark belt is very fragile, so I asked Cliff Bell, a local artisan in leather art and design, to make a replica for me to take back to the tribal lands. Cliff copied the design and measurements exactly on to a thick strip of grey suede. At my request, he also made a second Grade Belt to my design for the Chief as a gift. This belt combined the sacred symbols of the Isle of Man and Tanna Island, namely the triskele and boar's tusks. The triskele was positioned in the centre of the belt and the boar's tusks supporting it on either side along the length of the belt.

Interestingly, now that we have powerful telescopes, we can see that spiral galaxies are in the form of the triskele. Does this sacred symbol indicate the home world of the Star People who first came to Tanna Island?

1st May 2012:
Red Dragon of London
There had been subtle evidence from different sources that the London Olympics, being held in July and August, were going to be targeted by terrorist agencies. In view of this possibility, I called upon the Dragon of London City to stand guard over the ancient sites of our ancestors, long buried now under modern concrete. I journeyed shamanically into the lower world where I saw this magnificent red dragon, chained and manacled, imprisoned in a deep dungeon. It was very angry at being held against its will and didn't realise that the energy of this anger was holding its chains in position by strengthening their energy field. It took some time for me to calm the dragon down, calling in other dragons and their riders to support me. Eventually, after it realised that I was telling the truth and that as a Bearer of the Dragon Sword, I was to be trusted. It "surrendered" to me and became still. I instructed the dragon to call back its vital force from the chains and the surrounding dungeons to enable it to be fully present. As it did so, the chains fell away and the Red Dragon of London rose through the earth into the sunlight once again. It had been contained and manacled for generations by those who had magical knowledge used for the wrong reasons.

Now the Great Red Dragon of London was free, holding out its wings, cradling the City of London, calling to its rider and awakening the ancient Knights of Albion who are pledged to protect their homeland and their descendants. I had never encountered the ancient Knights of Albion before. Those I saw were mature men, not young warriors. They had the appearance of magicians (note: Albion is the true name of the kingdom we now know as England). We all come from a unique lineage of spiritual ancestors, which is different to our genetic ancestors.

During the weeks that followed until my departure to the tribal lands, I connected with the Kassoso and also with High Chief Wai Wai Rawi at the sacred nakamal fire. I didn't receive any great spiritual insights, rather I was keeping the channels of communication open between us and with Spirit. I had been given an impressive collection of smoking pipes, some very ornate and obviously expensive. These were a gift for the High Chief and the men at Itabu. Maggie gradually made up parcels for three females she worked with in the tribe, Namu, Nahu and Tuna, containing jewellery, cash and clothing. I also bought items to take for Liz in Port Vila that she couldn't obtain in Vanuatu. Liz had offered to put me up at her house to save expensive hotel costs.

In July, I gave a presentation about the tribe at the Penzance Literary Festival and also at the British Society of Dowsers Annual Conference in September, leaving immediately afterwards for Vanuatu. I left the Isle of Man on 26th September 2012, staying overnight at a bed and breakfast near to Gatwick Airport for an early departure the following day to Singapore, via Dubai.

28th September 2012:
Singapore

I arrived in Singapore on time; I had no difficulty passing through customs and immigration, then things went downhill! The taxi driver got lost trying to find my hotel, a lodge between the airport and the city. Next door to the hotel were kennels and an adventure centre for dogs (yes, really!). Some of the advertised activities for the dogs were: etiquette lessons, health checks, bakery, grooming, shop, day care, gym and sports activities, massage, swimming (with life jackets) and career choices (!). They called these kennels "The Dogmatory". During the day, there was constant barking from countless dogs, people shouting and the occasional small dog screaming as a big dog shook it like a rat, thinking it was a snack.

My hotel room was windowless. Rooms with a window are classed as a luxury, so more money was required to have a room with a view. I felt exhausted, so bought some bread from a local bakery for my dinner, losing a filling from one of my teeth, then slept.

30th September 2012:
Conflict of Three Oriental Dragons

I received the inner calling to connect with the Dragon of Singapore so went into meditation to do a shamanic journey to see what, if anything, the Dragon of Singapore needed me to do.

I connected to a typical Oriental dragon, which was dark jade green in colour, writhing in a turbulent sea fighting with another Oriental dragon, which initially looked red. On closer examination, I saw that the Jade Dragon of Singapore was in mortal combat with the Dragon of the Rising Sun of Japan! What I learned was that this conflict was still in active process since the invasion of Singapore by the Imperial Japanese Forces during the Second World War. I learned that the collective Japanese psyche of invoking their gods and archetypes (the dragon consciousness) to aid their war machine was still at war in a different realm of consciousness long after hostilities, physically, were over. No priest had retracted the Japanese Dragon (mindset) of invasion to conquer the Dragon of Singapore. The Jade Dragon of Singapore was still defending its homeland!

Also what was interesting was that I saw a third dragon, a purple one this time, also Oriental in nature, which was the Dragon of Malaysia and Burma, which had been supressed and trapped by the Dragon of the Rising Sun. In essence, three Oriental dragons were in conflict, therefore, this would still have a destabilising effect on this region of Asia and the Orient.

After assessing which dragon was the principal one needing work, I found that I needed to withdraw the Dragon of the Rising Sun and return it to Japan so that the other two could begin to stabilise and balance their worlds. I called upon the dragon consciousness of Japan and asked it to call back its missing soul part from this region of Singapore, which it did instantly. Calmness and peace descended upon the area and a deep sleep ensued, to enable inner healing to begin in this region.

In the afternoon, there was heavy thunder, lightning and rain. The dogs next door began to bay and cats nearby began to wail. It was really quite awesome.

1st October 2012:
Ronnie's nakamal

Today I left Singapore for the long-haul flight to Brisbane, Australia. The flight took about seven hours and I arrived in the early hours of 2nd October. After going into the transit lounge at Brisbane Airport, I had almost ten hours to wait for the flight to Port Vila, via Santo. Espiritu Santo Island (Spanish for Holy Spirit) is the largest island in the Vanuatu archipelago. Everybody calls it simply Santo.

I arrived at the capital Port Vila, which is on Efate Island, at about 4 p.m. Immigration and Customs facilities had all been changed and modernised since my last visit. The colourful island string band that traditionally played and sang for arriving visitors and tourists was no longer permitted to greet people at immigration but their distant voices were heard in the arrival hall.

Liz had sent her business driver Joel to pick me up and take me to her business address, where we met face to face for the first time. After a brief rest, we went on to Liz's house, where I was greeted by Anna, Liz's helper who was also staying with Liz temporarily. I was shown to my room and, after a refreshing shower and a change of clothes, Liz and I headed off on foot to Ronnie's nakamal, which was a couple of blocks away from where Liz lived to drink kava, the traditional South Pacific medicine plant. Ronnie's nakamal was a meeting place for expats, who gathered at dusk to drink kava and chat. The nakamal was not like the Chief's at Itabu but more of a meeting place, minus the sacred ceremony. I was introduced to other expat friends, principally Australians, New Zealanders and British. Liz seemed to be part of a little group who met and sat at their preferred table.

One of the girls I was introduced to was Manx and her mother knew Maggie. Liz drank several coconut shells of kava. I just drank one. It didn't feel right to drink kava without doing the correct ritual. It felt disrespectful somehow. Unlike the preparation of kava at the Itabu nakamal, where the root is masticated and spat out into a leaf and water added, the kava in Vila was crushed by a machine. It was weak compared to the kava at Itabu.

Michael, the Chief's nephew, was in Port Vila at this time, so Liz had organised that he would come to Ronnie's nakamal to meet me. Michael sported a slight beard, which surprised me, as traditionally only chiefs and yeramanus (shamans) are permitted facial hair in southern Tanna. Michael explained he was going to New Caledonia to stay with family during my visit to Itabu, so would not be available to act as interpreter this time. This was disappointing. Michael brought me up to date with events and news from Itabu since my last visit in 2010. Nikwei, the Yeramanu at Itabu had moved back to Lenakel, the capital town of Tanna Island, as he had been living with the Chief for several years. His family in Lenakel was complaining that he never tended to his land properly. He has built a new house there now but is expected back at Itabu soon.

Donald, the Chief's firstborn son, who will inherit the position of High Chief at his father's death, has a new baby daughter. His kitchen house burnt to the ground and he lost everything that he owned (I already knew this from the Chief's letter). Jack, the Chief's second born son, is married and has a child. Nahu, the Chief's second oldest daughter, is still not married. Michael laughed, raising his eyebrows, saying, 'She is too strong, men are afraid of her!'

Enoch, the Chief's third born son, has moved out of Itabu and lives in a village on the far side of the volcanic ash plain. Tuna, the Chief's youngest daughter, is betrothed to be married. Fred, the voodoo priest, is dead because of black magic used against him. He really was not a nice person.

A cyclone did a lot of damage at Itabu earlier and demolished the toilet and wash huts. Michael also said that the authorities had temporarily closed Yasur volcano to all visitors, as it is now too dangerous.

Michael and I arranged to meet in town the following day, since I had some supplies to buy before I left for Tanna Island. Michael disappeared into the darkness and Liz and I walked back to her house.

3rd October 2012:
Shopping for Supplies   Death of a Girl

I woke at 4 a.m. and was unable to get back to sleep. It usually takes me about four days to get over jetlag. Once I can stand up with bare feet on the earth, I would be able to ground myself better. Modern synthetic fabrics and shoes in particular disconnect us from the natural electromagnetic influences of the planet, so have the effect of causing imbalances in our own electromagnetic fields.

I met Michael in town and gave him some money to get credit on his mobile phone to call the Chief. Michael told the Chief I still wore my ear stick after the last initiation in 2010, which pleased him. The Chief also conveyed that the Tokka Festival was now set for next week, so I could attend. Michael said that the Chief thought this was a good omen for my visit and that he was really excited at my return home.

In the daylight, I could see that Michael had several new tattoos, including one under his right eye. He said that traditionally families had a peculiar tattoo mark which the community recognised, as well as grade tattoos. He said that Nahu had had new tattoos as well. Michael said that a young girl at Itabu, a member of the Chief's family, had died yesterday from some sort of sickness, so the Chief was overseeing the funerary arrangements that day and the next. It is a very sad time when a child dies.

Michael disappeared to do what he needed to do so I changed some money into Vatu, the Vanuatu currency, reconfirmed local flights at the Air Vanuatu office, and got some supplies for Tanna Island, such as tobacco, lighters, things of that nature. Port Vila had changed drastically in the two years that I had been away. A lot of people, especially expats, drove quad bikes, which are now a very common form of transport, but most people still drive like old Manx farmers – all over the road, no indication and vehicles totally unroadworthy.

In the evening, at dusk, Liz and I went up to Ronnie's nakamal again for the evening kava. All the expat friends around our table agreed it was much stronger tonight.

I was looking forward, at long last, to experiencing the Tokka Festival, also known as Nekowiar ceremony. This ceremony or festival brings together neighbouring villages for three days and nights of gift-giving ceremonies, kastom dances and feasting. The main Tokka ceremony is considered a most impressive traditional dance.

12th October 2012:
Chief badly hurt in Road Accident   Kastom Healing

I had my first good night's rest and sleep since leaving home. Liz arranged transport for me to the airport and my flight to Tanna Island. The authorities at the domestic terminal say that travellers are only permitted one suitcase, or equivalent and one piece of cabin baggage, yet most of the local people were checking in for the flight to Tanna Island with cargo. One family had 22 pieces of baggage in various shapes and sizes, including gardening tools. Tourists were dutifully checking in one piece of luggage.

There was a government promotional video being played in the terminal lounge about various custom (kastom) traditions of Vanuatu. Part of the Tanna clip showed Yasur volcano and High Chief Wai Wai Rawi and the men of Itabu performing the nambas (penis sheath) dance. My heart warmed when I saw my brother.

Our flight was delayed because of the amount of cargo that needed packing so we arrived at White Sands Airport near Lenakel a little late. I was delighted to see the Chief waving to me at the back of the waiting crowd. I pushed my way through the mêlée to embrace my brother and saw to my horror that his right arm was in a sling and his hand wrapped in a bloody bandage. There was also fresh blood on his shirt.

'What happened!' I exclaimed, putting my arm around his shoulder to comfort him. Tears welled up in his eyes.

The Chief explained that he had hired a truck to take him to the airport to meet me and also to pick up some tourists, when they were hit virtually broadside by another truck which failed to stop and give way at an intersection on the dirt road beyond the ash plain. As vehicles are left-hand drive in this country, the Chief received the full impact of the crash, throwing him out of his seat and across the driver. Both vehicles were extensively damaged so the driver called the police on his cell phone. The Chief was taken to hospital by a passing truck where they diagnosed several broken bones in his right hand and had attempted to treat the split flesh. The Chief complained more about the pain in his wrist and also his shoulder and neck. I was shocked at the state and appearance of my brother; he was clearly in great distress and looked old and tired beyond his years. His hair had turned whiter and his eyes looked bloodshot and the whites yellow (I hoped he wasn't one of the men preparing and chewing kava, as I didn't relish hepatitis flavoured phlegm and saliva).

I collected my bag and we waited in the truck for the tourists, a couple who were staying at a new lodge not far from Itabu. They were duly found and their bags loaded into our truck. The driver and the Chief sat in the front and the three of us in the rear seats. My companions were a local boy from Port Vila and an Asian girl; they kissed and cuddled most of the way to Itabu, which was not the done thing in Vanuatu. The Chief was clearly uncomfortable with it. They found the bumpy, dusty journey difficult and complained when a passing truck filled the vehicle with swirling red dust from the open window. He covered his face with a handkerchief and coughed like a true thespian on the stage. He pulled his girlfriend closer to him so she protected him from the worst of the dust.

State and local government had engaged an international contractor to excavate and construct a new highway from Lenakel all the way to Port Resolution. It was a huge and costly undertaking and very destructive, as bulldozers smashed down trees, uprooting them and pushing them aside like matchwood. I felt sick when I saw it. Not only that, they would be interfering with the tribal spirit highways, graves (which are often seen at the side of the road) and changing traditional tribal boundaries, long ago fought over in violent battles ending in cannibal feasts. I know that once this highway reaches Itabu that will be the end of a simple way of life, gone forever, extinct. For some reason, gangs of workers were constructing the highway in sections along its proposed route so, when we arrived at a newly concreted section, the drive was smooth and dust free.

We stopped at one construction roadblock to allow heavy plant to move loads of dumped aggregate. The trucks hauling the stone were literally scrap on wheels, often breaking down. As we waited in the heat to be waved on, a swarm of flies came into our truck, causing "City Boy" to flap his hands around his head, covering his face with his shirt. His girlfriend laughed at him for being so precious, which didn't go down very well. They were looking forward to getting to their air-conditioned, four star, luxury lodge. I smiled at the thought that there was no such place, amused at what their reaction would be when they arrived at a bush lodge.

We passed over Snake Hill, so called because the road meanders up and over the steep mountain pass, where we could see Yasur volcano belching out black smoke on the ash plain below. The tourists were excited and "City Boy" began to complain of what would happen if the volcano exploded in the night and they were all killed. I suggested that he would make a suitable sacrifice to the local gods. He glared at me; the Chief sniggered in the front seat.

We arrived at the tourist lodge, recently built, which hadn't been there two years ago. It was the usual standard construction, made of local materials, including thatched tree houses. The only way to reach the tree houses was up steep, shaky ladders. We dropped off their bags and left them standing at the side of the road, clearly shocked at their primitive accommodation.

We passed Iaqurimano school, which had its roof ripped off in places from a cyclone in 2004. These holes had been covered for years by a blue tarpaulin. Now the school had a new blue tin roof that shone in the sunlight. Children playing nearby the dirt road ran towards us, shouting and waving as our truck passed.

We arrived at Itabu where the Chief's family and the whole village had turned out to greet the return of their injured High Chief. He had phoned ahead to let Donald know about the accident. Donald had informed the rest of the family. The Chief stumbled out of the truck into the embrace of his family who were crying and clearly distressed. Glenda, the Chief's third eldest daughter, had travelled to Itabu from her village across the valley when she heard about her father's accident. She held him close and sobbed into his shoulder, gently stroking his bloodied hand. The Chief was overcome with emotion as all around him cried, some loudly. I felt alienated because I sensed I was the cause of this predicament. I sat quietly in the shade of a thatched hut to observe the situation and to wait to be called forward. It was the Chief's time now, not mine.

I was called by the Chief and we held each other; the others then greeted me. The women, especially Namu, Donald's wife, wanted to know where Natu (Maggie) was. I explained that she could not come this time. Namu uncovered a small baby from under her clothes, explaining it was her new baby girl whom she had named Natu after my wife. I was deeply touched by this honour.

The leaf hut I stayed in. My grade belt is hanging over the tree stump

I was shown to my leaf hut, recently built on a rise overlooking the village. In the local tradition, fresh flowers, especially hibiscus, were laid at the threshold and on the pillows of my bed. As I was unpacking my bag I heard more activity and commotion in the village, so looked out of my window to see a group of women gathering like startled starlings. I left my hut and went down to see what was happening. Jack, the Chief's second born son, had arrived with a white plastic chair, which the Chief now sat in. The women suddenly formed a circle around the Chief and began to sway and wail until they reached a point of resonance with their voices which had the effect of a group of people chanting or toning in synchronised unison. It was truly amazing and I could feel my body vibrating as energy moved through it.

One of the women, who appeared to be the leader, and I guessed this was her kastom lineage, began to sing in a harmonious way, face skywards, swaying, seemingly in a trance-like state offering prayers to Majikjiki and to the ancestors. As the energy built by the wailing women, they spontaneously began to place their hands on the Chief's body. This had the effect of giving the Chief permission to wail with them to release his deep trauma. The wailing women then stopped and broke up. One of them fetched a container of water which she poured over his arm and hand, presumably to reduce inflammation, pain and swelling. Two other elderly women pulled off the Chief's shirt and began to massage his upper body, neck and shoulders with coconut oil. I was surprised at how rough they were. Another younger woman moved behind the Chief and started pulling his head roughly in different directions – upwards and side to side – which appeared to be some sort of traction adjustment. The Chief grimaced and moaned with pain. Then several men and older women came forward, chewing a certain leaf which was obviously kastom medicine, spraying the contents of their mouths on to the Chief's wounds in particular but also the upper body and head.

I looked around at all of those gathered; some still cried, tears falling from their cheeks on to the dark earth; others stared with blank expressions. Men frowned and spoke softly amongst themselves, almost in reverence. What united all of these souls was a deep love and respect for their High Chief. I was genuinely touched by their sense of community.

People then began to disperse. It seemed that the healing was over. After the kastom healers had left, the Chief told me it was time to go to the nakamal. I went ahead with Jack. The Chief went to change his bloodied shirt. Jack and I started to gather wood from the forest for the nakamal fire and then the heavens opened, so we ran for cover under the banyan tree to shelter from the heavy rain. The tropical downpour lasted only a few minutes, then the sun came out and shone again. In seconds the black volcanic earth was steaming.

The Chief and Donald arrived with a small pig and kava roots. The pig and kava were to be used in a ceremony to help the healing of the Chief's injuries. I was told by one of the men lighting the sacred fire that the Chief had been telling them for many days that 'my brother is coming.' He was really excited, the man said.

The men couldn't find the club for killing the pig; it was always kept in the aerial roots of the banyan tree. I was instructed by the Chief to hold the pig down whilst Donald bludgeoned it to death with a large stone – not ideal. The pig was then butchered at the perimeter of the nakamal, whilst others cut spiked sticks to cook its flesh and organs over the fire. Another fire was lit; this was the first time I had seen two fires lit at the nakamal. Because the wood was wet from the tropical downpour, the fires gave off copious amounts of thick white smoke which stung our eyes and did a thorough job of smudging us. I looked around the familiar nakamal and noticed that the forest had been cleared and several new leaf huts had been built with pig enclosures. Nothing stays the same.

The Chief spoke to me after everyone was settled, saying that he had had a dream last night that he was going to be involved in a car accident! I wondered what the significance of this was spiritually. The Chief asked me for some healing. By this time there were twelve assembled men, so I called in the ancestors as I had been taught by the Chief. The Chief asked me to remove his shoes and socks as he wanted to feel the dark earth beneath his bare feet. I massaged the reflexology pressure points on his feet, corresponding to his hand, wrist, arm, shoulder and neck. All proved tender.

For years, I have been wearing a feather in my hairband; today was no exception.
I had a black and white chicken feather in my hair, which I had moved to do some
feather extraction work on the Chief's hand and wrist. After finishing, I passed the
feather through the thick white smoke of the fire to cleanse it, then put it back onto
my hair. The Chief looked at me and said, 'Why do you wear that feather in your
hair? It is not kastom. Take it out."

This was not a request by the High Chief but a command. I removed the feather.
The Chief went on to explain that I was only permitted to wear an eagle feather or
the black tail feathers of a rooster. Likewise, he added, Natu was only permitted to
wear the white tail feathers of a rooster, none other.

One of the men preparing the kava blew his nose loudly into his hand, wiping the
slime on his trousers, then continued cleaning the kava root. The Chief and I were
called by Donald to take kava. We were given a coconut shell each by Donald, who
bowed gracefully. All of the men fell silent. We stood side by side as equal brothers,
drinking the kava in the usual ritual fashion, spraying the dregs on to the ground,
shouting, 'Tamaffa' to honour the spirit of this sacred temple space. The kava was
prepared to be very strong to help the Chief, as one of its sacred qualities is as an

Preparing kava.
Donald spits out
the masticated
kava into a leaf
"plate", ready to
add water.

analgesic. The man who blew his nose into his hand then brought me one of the pig's kidneys, which had been roasting on the fire, to eat after the kava. The Chief spoke softly as the other men drank their kava, explaining that the Kassoso were wild men, so there was no guarantee that they would show up when asked and could simply arrive when you least expected it.

The men gathered around the Chief and asked him to tell them the full story about his accident. Again, this was interesting. As the Chief relayed the story, it was another means of releasing the trauma, but also to validate his experience in a sacred space. The men kept referring to me as Apu, meaning elder or wise man. I ate more pig flesh, burnt black on the outside and raw in the middle, but refused a second shell of kava. I didn't want to be disgraced in public by vomiting.

The Chief said he was delighted with me still wearing my ear stick and said this was powerful medicine for connecting with the Kassoso. I smiled inwardly, as he still didn't have one himself! Some of the other men wore ear sticks or had long pieces of grass or feathers through their ears.

For some reason, the Chief had recently shaved off his beard and what had grown back was white, scruffy and patchy. I said to him that I wasn't sure if I were to regrow my beard after the shaving ritual in 2010 or to stay clean-shaven, so to be safe, I grew it again. Besides, I added, Natu told me not to come home without it! The Chief laughed. He said that the Kassoso were not pleased with him for shaving it off. He still didn't say why he had done it. I joked with the Chief and said that, now he had a broken hand, I would have to put his nambas on for him. He laughed and said that his left hand was his best!

I returned to the new "restaurant" which was being built during my last visit. Nahu had cooked a meal consisting of more bush pig, rice, noodles and onions. I really enjoyed it. I didn't feel nauseous or dizzy this time after drinking the kava. I was very thankful for this.

I made my way up to the steep rise in the darkness after my meal by lantern light, which cast eerie shadows amongst the tropical foliage. My heart felt glad to be back in the tribal lands beneath the clear night skies, lit with a red glow from Yasur volcano and the fireflies chasing each other through the tree canopies. The flying foxes called to each other as they foraged for fruit. I climbed, tired and exhausted, into my bed.

5th October 2012:

Strawberry Jam   Sacred Skulls   Cannibalism

I didn't sleep well last night. By 5:30 am, the villagers were already up and about at first light beginning their chores. Their constant laughter seemed to carry through the rain forest. Compared with my last visit, the village was quiet, no barking dogs or crowing roosters. I hung my Grade Belt over a rotten tree stump by my hut to absorb the elements and energy of the tribal lands.

At 6 am, I went for a cold shower. There was no door on the shower hut, except for a piece of cloth that hung down from the door frame, which blew horizontally in the high winds. I hooked it over a couple of protruding nails at the bottom of the door.

Itabu had changed beyond recognition since my last visit. All of the old leaf huts and restaurant were demolished and new huts built in different places. The old toilet and shower block had been flattened by a recent cyclone and had been rebuilt, and the old porcelain toilet pan smashed. The new toilet was a high, angled, rectangular box, with a narrow hole cut in the top, placed over a squat latrine. You straddled this device as it you were mounting a horse. I was intrigued by everyone's clothes lines, strung throughout the village on long poles. The lines were actually barbed wire and the clothes were simply impaled on to the barbs to dry. No item of clothing broke free in the high winds – that was guaranteed. The only problem was that everybody's clothes were holed and torn, which was a slight disadvantage.

I was called for breakfast at 7 am. Breakfast consisted of Ceylon tea from Fiji and locally baked bread from Lenakel, with a new jar of strawberry jam, made in Pakistan; on reading the label about the ingredients, it stated "nature identical strawberry flavour" (plus serious chemicals). This reminded me of the time we were travelling through Algeria in 1973. We pulled up outside an abandoned French Colonial Administrative Complex at the edge of the Sahara Desert where, within the courtyard and high walls, long plain wooden trestle tables were laid out for the local people who wanted breakfast. All there was on offer was bread and jam. Our group sat amongst the local Arabs and helped ourselves after paying the fee. Bread was laid on the bare table boards and huge tins of strawberry jam were spaced out between everyone. We were enjoying our feast until I noticed that the Arab sitting next to me was picking out the strawberries and lining them up along the rim of his plate. Fascinated, I leaned over to get a closer look and, to my horror, saw they were actually large bluebottles which had been processed and canned along with the jam. I wondered why the jam had a mild crunch.

As I finished breakfast, Donald arrived and took me to his hut where the Chief was sitting on a woven pandanus mat on the earth, waiting for me. As a shamanic practitioner, I did some energy work with him to aid his healing process; then we both returned to the restaurant to talk.

The majority of people, including healers themselves, seem to misunderstand the true nature of what healing is. It is not a cure-all. True healing is where the practitioner aids the client, through an exchange of energy, to assist the client to correct imbalances for themselves, which may mean that the condition they are experiencing becomes worse as toxins are released and deep trauma held in the fascia comes to the surface. They are forced to face their fears. The greatest form of healing, of course, is aiding the death journey.

I had difficulty in understanding the Chief fully, which was the usual practice for the first couple of days. Then we fell into a routine where we could understand each other with ease, with a little help from others. The Chief said he wanted me to ask him questions that I needed answering. I was grateful for this opportunity to clarify and learn more about the tribe's culture.

We spoke of many things, such as the tribal creation myth; Kassoso; Tokka Festival; cannibalism and sacred skulls. The Chief explained that the kastom tradition of Tanna Island originated with his ancestors at Itabu, then moved gradually northwards. This included the wearing of nambas, the penis sheath. In the Itabu area, these sheaths are made of hibiscus fibres rolled into a long phallic shape, where the penis is either tied tightly between the rolled fibres and the belly or tied inside the roll. It is a symbol of virility and fertility. All males wore these sheaths until the missionaries began banning the tradition. The exception to this, he said, was Kassoso, who always stay at the volcano and, until recently, Majikjiki who seems now to have become a national hero and god.

The Chief said he would reveal more of the secret stories little by little during my stay. The Chief continued that, when he first met me in 2003, he had a dream where the ancestors instructed him to initiate me as a Chief, so he prepared and drank a sacred type of kava, rarely used except under special circumstances, known locally as tabunga. The spiritual insights and instructions he received after taking this sacred root gave him permission to reveal to me the tribal secrets, to undergo initiations and to give to me my tribal name, Iarueri, meaning the first one or god. He took the same sacred root to find the true name for Maggie, which was Natu Elin, meaning High Woman of good repute.

We spoke about the sacred skulls. The Chief reminded me that I was from the lineage of the Guardians of the Ancestral Skulls, as was confirmed to him in a dream which he wrote to me about some time ago. The Chief said that, in his tribal

When I was in Papua, New Guinea in 1983, I went to Aseki, a remote highland village where I spent some time studying the tribal ancestral skulls and bodies kept in baskets in a cave in the mountains overlooking the village.

culture, at death the skull was not separated from the corpse but the whole body was deeply buried to stop the pigs from digging it up to eat. However, he continued, the removal of the skulls and the big leg bones was carried out on Erromango Island, a neighbouring island to Tanna and their traditional enemies. Tannese fishermen, who drowned at sea were often washed up on the beaches of Erromango, he said, where their skulls and leg bones were collected and stored. Since I was a boy, I have always held a deep fascination about the ritual and ceremony around human skulls and cannibalism. Is it ancient cellular memory?

When I was in Papua, New Guinea in 1983, I went to Aseki, a remote highland village where I spent some time studying the tribal ancestral skulls and bodies kept in baskets in a cave in the mountains overlooking the village. I had an inner knowledge that I had already reconnected to sacred skull magic, so there was no need to do it any more. (I also trained as a post mortem technician, specialising in opening skulls.)

After about an hour, the Chief excused himself as he was still in great pain and needed to rest. His hand and fingers were swollen, like a balloon. He hadn't slept either. I gave my brother the smoking pipes and tobacco for distribution and some money to pay for his hospital treatment. I also presented to him the Grade Belt that I had had made for him. He was delighted with it.

I returned to my hut to collect some dirty clothes which I washed in a bowl outside the toilet block, draping them over a rope washing line at the back of my hut to dry in the sun. No barbed wire for me!

For some reason, I started to feel mildly ill with flu-like symptoms developing further throughout the day. With the Chief injured now, it would change what was planned regarding ceremony and travel between villages. I felt disappointed, but knew that whatever I was meant to experience would be so. I spent the rest of the day resting and trying to connect with Kassoso.

I was called to go to the nakamal at 4 pm, as usual. We passed through Donald's little encampment, now extended with more huts, gardens and pig pens. Kipson, Donald's youngest son, came out of one of the leaf huts, playing with a broken knife. We arrived at the nakamal, where boys were already preparing the kava. Older boys and youths were playing marbles.

The Chief arrived and asked me for some more healing. After the session, we sat on a log to talk. He explained that, as a child preparing kava in the older days, he remembered 40 or more men gathered each evening at the nakamal, all dressed in nambas. Now, he said sadly, only a few came and they were all dressed in Western clothes, which the Kassoso dislike. The Chief looked directly into my eyes and said, 'Brother, can you write down the stories I tell you, so when I have died a record still lives on?'

I hadn't told him yet about the book I had written "Return of the White Serpent" doing just that. This was confirmation and verification for me that I was doing the ethical thing to help the Chief.

The Chief went on to talk about cannibalism. 'We used to fight and kill each other, then eat the men like eating a pig. The white man and missionaries came and gave some men guns, so the balance of tribal warfare was lost. It became murder for the sake of it. As a boy, I remember the old men in the nakamal talking about the men they had eaten.'

Then the Chief changed the subject without warning to the forthcoming Tokka Festival. 'The Tokka will be held in a few days. All of the women dancers should be bare-breasted, wearing only a grass skirt. The men dancers should be naked, except for nambas.'

Other men gathered around us to listen to our conversation. One man asked me how long it had taken me to travel from Manannan's Island (Isle of Man) to Tanna Island. I told him that, on this occasion, it took me seven days. I also told the men the approximate cost of travel in Vatu, their local currency, so they had some understanding of my commitment and financial outlay. They found this incredible and all started whistling. Some slapped their heads with their hands and rolled their eyes. I was asked questions about Manannan's Island and the Celtic culture.

The Chief and I were called to drink kava together. It was very strong again to help ease the Chief's pain. After drinking, I stumbled back to my log by the fire, wide-eyed and rocking like an imbecile. My brain felt as if it was on fire and my eyes felt as though they were under great pressure and wanted to explode outwards. I became dizzy, but not nauseous this time, thankfully. I was given some rice to eat, presented on a leaf plate.

After the kava, all the men fell into silence for their prayers to the ancestors, to Majikjiki and Kassoso. The Chief brought out a selection of the smoking pipes and tobacco I had brought, much to the delight of the assembled men. All sat in silent prayer, staring into the flickering flames of the sacred fire, occasionally drawing on their pipes, then offering the smoke back into the flames. It was very powerful and peaceful, except for the occasional explosion of the volcano, the chirping of the

Natonga Kwat
(Donald) holding
a flying fox,
caught to eat.

cicadas and the chattering of the flying foxes. The flying foxes fulfil many important roles, spiritually and physically, for the tribe. When the bats eat fruit, they spread the seeds and stones in their droppings all over the forest so that plants and trees may grow to produce more fruit for the benefit of all.

I returned to the restaurant for my evening meal of fish, rice and vegetables, then fell into my bed.

6th October 2012:
Kastom Doctor   Kassoso   Leaf Hut

I had another sleepless night due to persistent biting mosquitoes, the effects of strong kava and the flu-like symptoms which persisted for some reason. I finally got some rest in the early hours of the morning until I was woken by someone raking up fallen leaves outside my leaf hut at 5 o'clock in the morning. It was dawn, so time to get up and to greet the sun.

I stuck my head out of the door to see the black and scarlet majikjiki bird (cardinal honeyeater) flitting from flower to flower. By my door was a rotten tree stump and I noticed for the first time that a very large yellow hornet had started to build its nest there. We eyeballed each other and made the mutual agreement that neither of us would trespass into each other's house. I was fascinated by its colour and beauty.

Suddenly, someone began to play the tam tam drum (wooden slit drum). It sounded too far away to be the one at Itabu. I heard women wailing, which at first sounded like a pack of baying wolves. It was remarkable and somewhat scary! Their cries seemed to carry in the early morning mist that floated through the jungle. I wondered if some ceremony was being performed for the Chief, or was it totally unrelated and someone had died perhaps? In any case, I had not been invited, so it wasn't my place to go noseying in case whatever was happening was private or secret. You have to be very careful with tribal cultures that you do not trespass into a situation where you could get yourself killed.

I washed and went to the restaurant for breakfast. Nahu was nowhere to be seen, so I guessed she was involved in some way, as she was the Chief's oldest daughter still residing at Itabu. She had left a flask of hot water for me and a jar of "nature identical" jam. I found some hard breakfast crackers in the kitchen area, commonly referred to as dog biscuits.

The Chief arrived, looking exhausted, distressed and weary. His shirt and bandage were soaked in fresh blood. His hand was a bloody mess. He sat down heavily, wiping the sweat from his face. He looked dreadful. I waited for him to speak to give him time to catch his breath. I felt real concern for my brother. In essence, I felt sick and wondered if I had agreed at some level to share his distress by helping him carry this burden? Maybe this was what the unexpected flu-like symptoms were and I was helping him process his pain?

Nahu arrived and the Chief asked her for a mug so he could have some tea. This seemed to help him. He clearly wanted to talk about something and I was poised ready. The Chief began to describe the healing session he had just received from the kastom medicine man or doctor, a healer from a long tribal lineage in this part of the island. The tam tam called the kastom healer and supporting women to Itabu, where the Chief relayed the following story. 'I was laid down on a pandanus mat in the lower nakamal and the women began to gather. Then they started to wail around me. I couldn't stop myself from crying. The healers chewed a kastom leaf, then spat the juice on to my hand and arm. Men arrived and held me down, whilst the kastom doctor cut my wrist deeply to the bone with a bamboo knife to release the trapped bad blood and any bad spirits. I could see the broken ends of the bones in my own wrist. He pulled my hand and fingers to straighten the bones and to set them straight for the ends to rejoin, then sprayed more kastom plant juice on to the bones before closing the flesh and bandaging it. Iarueri, the cut was deep, about an inch long. It is important to release the bad blood so it can run out, otherwise the wound will rot. You could die. I had the same thing done when I broke my left leg some time ago. Western doctors can't help me now, only the kastom doctor. I might go back to the hospital for them to check me later? Kassoso and Majikjiki came to me in a dream last night and told me that this had to be done today at dawn.'

'You will see,' the Chief continued as he waved his arm in the air, 'that in a week's time my hand will be fine. The Western medicine will keep me sick. This process is the same for all broken bones, including the skull. White man's tablets are no good. Kastom medicine is needed to release the bad blood from bones that has got into the flesh. It is not meant to be there, so needs to be cleaned out, otherwise you will never heal properly.'

The Chief went on to say that, if I were to break any bone whilst at Itabu, the same ceremony would be done to me. Note to self: do not fracture any bones at Itabu!

The Chief looked and sounded brighter after the Ceylon tea from Fiji. He didn't touch the nature identical jam though. The Chief seemed high on adrenalin now and continued, 'Kassoso came to me in the night but they were too far away. They told me that Iarueri had to stay at Itabu for a month before they would allow you to touch them.'

I explained that this was impossible and I couldn't do this. The Chief said that he would talk to Kassoso and explain this to them and ask them if they would come to me during my stay at Itabu. He added that Kassoso didn't like the Western life style with such things as clothes, boots, radio noise, watches, etc. They prefer men naked, like themselves – no body sprays, perfumes or soap smells. 'We will ask them tonight at the nakamal to come to you and what do they need to eat – a pig or a black chicken? They live in Yasur volcano. This is their house, so this is why we do not like tourists to go there. The volcano is sacred ground and taboo for others. We may have to stop washing and then wipe our body with leaves to remove the stink of soap. Iarueri, it is very hard to touch the Kassoso. Remember, they can kill a man. When they touch you, you can go unconscious, so you need someone with you to use kastom medicine to bring you out of it. Kassoso are "secret men". They hate the church and its lies, turning people away from their kastom way of life. Ladies cannot go near the Kassoso during their moon time, otherwise they are OK.'

The Chief looked at me with compassion and love, as only twins could understand. 'Iarueri, I am going to tell you a secret. When I first met you, it was Kassoso who came to me in the night and told me that I had to give you the "power". This is why I couldn't refuse. I couldn't tell the other men this, because it is secret, so I told them that it was either my father or the ancestors that told me to do this thing.'

Now I began to understand the sequence of all of my initiations over the last nine years. The Chief asked if I lived in a city or in the forest. I told him that I lived in a village in the country, where there were woods and open fields. He smiled at this and said, 'Kassoso won't come to a place where there is noise.'

'Do you have a nakamal?' he asked.

'No, brother,' I replied, 'I don't have one.'

This answer disappointed him. He frowned and asked, 'How will Kassoso find you if you have no nakamal?'

I didn't know what to say to that. I knew exactly what he was saying – that I had to create a nakamal with a place for the sacred fire; then Kassoso will come to Manannan's Island. I knew I had to do this to complete the connection between the Isle of Man and Tanna.

'We don't read or write,' the Chief said, 'we have to remember our stories,' pointing to his head.

I asked him about the ancient myths and stories that may have been told around the nakamal fires by the old men. Did he remember them? The Chief looked sad and lowered his head, shaking it. 'No, brother. These stories are lost for ever.'

I asked the Chief to describe Kassoso for me. He brightened up with this and said that Kassoso are very tall. Their bodies are black, except for the throat area, which is white. Their faces are red and they have red eyes (I am not permitted to elaborate on this phenomenon) and they always carry a sharp stick. When they come out of the volcano at dusk, they are in the form of men; then at dawn, they become flying foxes returning to the bat roosts, then on to the volcano along their path (spirit highway). This is why we take kava and kill a pig or a chicken at dusk to connect with the Dragon Men.

'We talk to Kassoso before we need to hunt flying foxes to get their permission. Then, after the kastom leaf has been put on the sacred stone at the base of nabanga (banyan tree), many come to be killed so that we can eat. This ceremony takes place in February. Kassoso have no ladies; all are male.'

I was going to ask how their numbers multiplied if they never bred, but suddenly had the insight that, when kastom men die, they join their ranks as this was their belief system.

'As I said before, Iarueri, Kassoso don't like the church, as they say that the sacred fires are Hell and a place of damnation. When I die, I will go to Yasur volcano to join my ancestors, for I know that the fires will purify me and take away that which is bad to leave that which is good. I will become changed, then become Kassoso myself. This is why people are naturally drawn to visit fires and volcanoes. They recognise they are visiting God. The church calls it Satan; they are liars. They twist the truth about fire so it becomes a place of fear they call Hell. It is a place of healing and transformation.'

I was startled at two things. Firstly, the simplicity of the truth of this statement and, secondly, the sophisticated words the Chief was using. On cue, Yasur volcano exploded, as if to agree with what had been discussed. The Chief smiled, then rose, placing his hand on my shoulder as he was about to leave. I told the Chief that I had a gift for him, presenting him with a copy of my book about him and I and the tribe called "Return of the White Serpent".

I knew he couldn't read but, like most tribal peoples, he receives a lot of information from images such as artwork or photographs. I showed him the design on the front cover of the book of the two entwined serpents coming out of a volcano, one white, the other black, explaining that they represented the two of us. The Chief whistled and slapped his head with his good hand.

Then I opened the book to show him the coloured photographs of the people and places around Itabu, but in particular his photograph in full tribal attire and also an image of Mitac, his deceased wife in full tribal attire. The Chief gently stroked the photograph of his wife, whistling again, muttering, 'Good, Iarueri, very good.'

He was lost in thought for a moment then looked at me with tears in his eyes. I knew he still missed Mitac very much. Now he had a small memento of her and his people.

The Chief said that he needed to sleep and rest now. He stopped and turned, 'Speak with Kassoso, my brother.' Then he left.

By 11 am, the earth was too hot to walk on in bare feet. I returned to my hut to connect with Kassoso. Once I had dropped into the right state of mind to begin a shamanic journey, I became aware of a boar tapping on the wooden door of my leaf hut. It wouldn't come in. I went to greet it at the threshold but it went to stand in a clearing in the sun. I followed it, then knelt before it to honour this magnificent creature. He stood about 4 feet at the shoulders, very angular body shape, very powerful. He was dark red in colour and had two very large golden curved tusks. I spent some time becoming familiar with him. Once this was completed, he began to move forward to what I can only describe as a portal of liquid energy, which materialised right in front of us. He had come to be my spirit guide.

He indicated for me to follow, which I did, feeling a sensation of passing through water, then out on the other side, where we were in fire inside Yasur volcano. I recognised a land bridge I had travelled along many times before, but this time I was at a deeper level and at a depth where we were in hot caverns, not the seas of magma. The boar ran down a tunnel, with me following, until we came to a cave which was full of volcanic fumes and smoke. I coughed and found this environment toxic. As I looked more clearly, I saw that the fumes and smoke were clearing and venting through a large opening high up the volcano above the tree canopy.

I filled my lungs with fresh air, then was startled as a large bat-like creature landed nearby, then another. These were the Kassoso! How exciting. However, because of the venting smoke, they did not notice me and walked past into a deeper recess of the cave structure. Two more of their kind arrived; the second one saw me. They were very tall and thin; all carried long pointed fighting sticks. They were principally black, but I could see the white collars and red faces. They looked half human and half bat. The Kassoso clearly wasn't happy that I was in their sacred space and lunged at me with its fighting stick, bearing his impressive fangs. He uttered a sharp bark several times, which soon caused the others to return and gather around me.

The pig and I stood silently. I was not afraid. I explained who I was and why I had come. This calmed them down. I asked for the opportunity to touch them so that I may receive their wisdom and knowledge. They barked and chatted anxiously around me. An older Kassoso arrived, who quietened the group and quickly assessed the situation, then raised his pointed stick and jabbed it into the palm of my right hand, causing it to bleed. He did the same to his right hand, then grasped our hands together that our blood may flow and merge. I felt as though I was shapeshifting into a Kassoso myself. My body became long, lean and strong; my limbs became agile with the ability to climb any vertical structure like a spider and, of course, to fly.

We launched ourselves out of the cave entrance into the evening twilight, running like crabs down the rugged slopes of the volcano, climbing trees and running across their canopies to the Itabu nakamal. I saw the Chief and others preparing kava and killing a pig. The Chief saw us. He was afraid, but said nothing to the others, offering to us the pig and kava, which we consumed. We stayed at the nakamal, then began a tour of surrounding villages and their nakamals, returning to our refuge in the volcano at dawn.

I came out of the meditation. I was thankful for this connection, as usually an energetic link is required before a physical one can be made. Usually when I come out of a shamanic journey, I am more sensitive to my immediate surroundings.

I looked around my leaf hut, taking in the details of its construction. My leaf hut was much larger on this visit. I think it must have been a family hut, vacated for my benefit. It was about 20 feet long and 12 feet wide, divided in two by a bamboo partition, containing three beds – one double, which I slept in. The hut was traditionally built out of hardwood and bamboo with a banana leaf thatch. It was on short stilts to avoid flooding in the wet season. The walls were double-skinned with plaited split bamboo and split hardwood palings. The floor was timber framed with large split bamboo poles, which acted as planks.

The pitched roof was constructed of large supporting hardwood poles with smaller ones in between, to which was attached a woven banana mat of leaves. Four windows and a door were built in to the sides, all open to the breeze, covered by suspended lava-lava (sarong) cloth of various colours and designs that acted like curtains. Plastic mosquito nets hung over two of the beds, including mine. The floor was covered in woven pandanus mats and the beds constructed of hardwood timber with thin foam mattresses over a woven mat. It was a veritable playground for lizards, spiders and insects. The older bamboo was breaking down from the activity of woodworm, which covered everything in dust.

Because of this type of construction, the hut withstands most of the cyclonic weather. The bigger buildings have openings at either end under the roof gables to allow the high winds to funnel through the building. Modern breeze block buildings have too much wind resistance and they collapse in cyclones.

Donald called to me early to go the nakamal, as the Chief wanted me to see the kastom doctor before he started his second treatment. We arrived at Donald's encampment to find the Chief sitting on a mat in the sun, with several people gathered around him. The kastom doctor was a young man who was very tall by local standards, wearing black shorts and a dirty yellow T-shirt which, interestingly, had a picture of the Virgin Mary on the front. He had very long fingernails, which were filthy, as all locals had, and displayed no hygiene procedures when working with open wounds and blood. Thinking about this, I realised I had never seen anyone, at any time, wash their hands at Itabu.

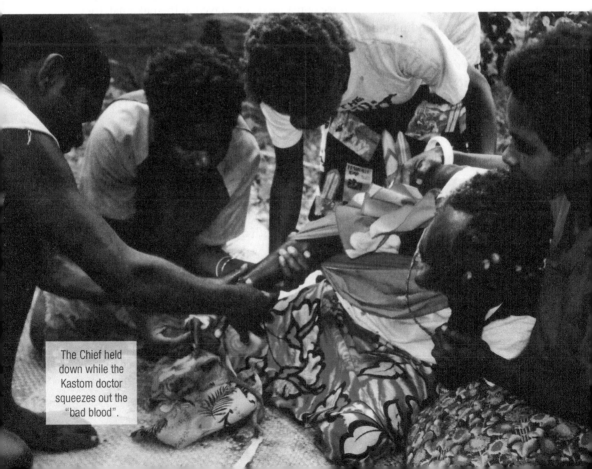

The Chief held down while the Kastom doctor squeezes out the "bad blood".

The filthy bandage was removed, most of which stuck to the wound and caused bleeding when pulled off. The kastom doctor squeezed the juice of a medicine plant over the wound to aid the bones to knit together. He indicated to those gathered around the Chief to hold him down. Namu, Nahu and others jumped on the Chief, pinning him to the ground, whilst others held his legs so he couldn't lash out. Still others held both arms. The kastom doctor was rough. He pulled apart the open wound and squeezed more kastom medicine on to the broken bones. The Chief cried out and more people piled on to him to keep him still. I felt sick. Then the kastom doctor started to squeeze the swollen tissue of the hand and broken fingers back into the gaping wound at the wrist to drain the area. The Chief screamed in agony. Tears rolled down his face, falling on to the mat.

The medicine man showed no compassion. He instructed the others to hold the Chief's injured arm tightly as he began to squeeze and push the gaping wound until it bled profusely, flushing out the old blood from the bones. This he kept referring to as the bad blood. The Chief was moaning and in agony; he seemed semi-conscious now. More kastom medicine was squeezed on to the wound as he pushed the flesh back together again. The kastom doctor told the women to put back the filthy bandage over the wound. He wiped his bloody hands on his shirt, laughed and then left.

The Chief was helped to sit up. Namu wiped the tears from his face. I wanted to cry at such brutal treatment to my brother. Namu and the other nursing mothers pulled out their breasts to feed their babies. I noticed they all shared the clothing and jewellery that I had given them as gifts from Natu. One woman straightened out the filthy bandage to wrap it around the open wound; others kept the flies away. I held my hand up and stopped them, indicating for them to wait until I had returned from my hut. I quickly grabbed a clean cotton shirt and some antiseptic spray I had brought for minor wounds and returned to my brother, who looked pale and weak. I tore my shirt into strips to the gasps of those around me and instructed them to change the bandage regularly and to wash the old ones with hot soapy water so they could be used again.

I knew what the Chief thought about Western medicine, so I offered the antiseptic spray to him as a choice. Another man, who could read English, scrutinised the contents of the spray to make sure it was compatible to kastom medicine. He declared it was, so I showed them how to shake the canister and to spray the antiseptic solution about 6 inches away in a broad spectrum. I indicated to keep the spray away from their eyes, children and any naked flame. The spray stung the wound, but the Chief was glad of it. The women bandaged his wrist and hand in a clean piece of cloth. We left the Chief, stretched out in the evening sun until he went to the nakamal for the kava ritual. Routine is a very important part of indigenous practice.

Several men and boys had gathered in the nakamal, some I hadn't seen before. One came up to me to chat; he spoke good English. We chatted about different kastom traditions. This man said that High Chief Wai Wai Rawi was the last of the true full High Chiefs. Then the Chief arrived. He sat next to me by the fire, looking exhausted. By this time, the kava had been prepared so another man, who I hadn't seen before, took a mouthful of kava and sprayed it on to the Chief's hand and wrist. Kava is also antiseptic.

Strangers told me that both the President and Prime Minister of Vanuatu came from Tanna Island. This is why they are improving the island's infrastructure by constructing the new highway. They also have plans to extend the airport runway to receive international flights from Australia.

I told the Chief about my dreaming connecting with the Kassoso earlier. He was delighted with what I had told him and encouraged me to inform him of all of my dreams and visions, this process being very important in their culture. Tribesmen would literally go to war if warfare was dreamt about. Donald called the Chief and I over to take kava. We stood side by side, calling to Kassoso to come – the Chief for healing and for me to share their wisdom and knowledge.

I returned to the restaurant for my dinner, then made my way by lantern light to my hut to sleep.

7th October 2012:

Cannibals   Chief arrested   Magic Stone   Eating Cats

The mosquitoes were very bad again last night. In the end, I had to unwrap the plastic mosquito net and pull it around me. The problem with this is that, when a tropical night is still, airless and stifling, the mosquito net prevents any breeze cooling you down, so you overheat and sweat profusely. There were several holes in the net, but the situation was drastically improved, enabling me to sleep. The flu-like symptoms had gone on to my chest now, so I had a hacking cough.

When I awoke in the morning, there was a large squashed cockroach in my bed. I don't know how it passed away, as these creatures are virtually indestructible. I was up at dawn. The morning air was clean and refreshing. Brown and yellow butterflies glided amongst the tropical flowers. "Silvereyes", small olive green birds with silver eyes, darted amongst the foliage. The dawn chorus had already begun some time ago. I found this fascinating as this is now recognised and known as bioacoustic resonance or bioacoustic diversity. It has been scientifically proven now that certain trees cannot unfurl their buds without the frequency of a blackbird's song pattern.

I went for breakfast at 7 am, after a shower. The Chief arrived for our question and answer session. His hand was badly swollen but at least he had a clean bandage on it. He spoke at length about the Tokka Festival and said that 400 pigs would be slaughtered, all laid out end to end in a line that would stretch for a kilometre.

I asked him more questions about cannibalism. It was obviously still a sensitive subject to raise, so I told the Chief about cannibalism in Scotland. The Chief, like all tribal peoples, loves stories, so I told him of what I remembered of Sawney Bean and his wife in Scotland who were cannibals in the 1600s. They attacked, robbed and ate their victims for many years. They lived in a deep cave on the coast and eventually had 14 children. They in turn, through incest, had children and their children again, through incest, had more children still. When eventually caught, it was estimated that the Bean Clan had killed and eaten over 1,000 people.

This story seemed to loosen the Chief up a little to tell his version, 'When I was a small boy helping to prepare kava in the nakamal, I used to listen to the stories that the old men told around the fire. When a man was caught, he was bound hand and foot, then hung from the wrists and ankles over a long pole, like a pig is today, which was carried by two men over their shoulders. When they arrived at the nakamal, they lodged the bound man in the roots of nabanga. A fire would be lit. The men would do a ceremony to open the road to Majikjiki for the spirit of the man to pass along safely. A pig was killed with a club and kava was prepared; then the man was brought from the tree and killed in the same way as the pig. Before the hunt, the women of the village would have prepared the earth oven so, after the man was killed, he was cut up into pieces and the meat wrapped in banana leaves in the usual way. It took three to five hours to cook a man. When the meat was cooked, the Chief was the only person allowed to have the head and the heart. Everybody else ate what they wanted. In Tanna, women and children were not eaten. If there was warfare, any captured women would be kept for bearing children and being workers around the village. Different islands have separate traditions. In Malekula, they ate children, cutting them up and skewering the meat over the fire, like we cook the pigs here today.'

The Chief had clearly had enough about cannibalism so went on to other subjects. 'About the time of independence for Vanuatu (1980), the church tried to stamp out all of our kastom traditions. I was arrested and handcuffed by police for wearing nambas. I was taken to a police station in Lenakel, but I was supported by all of the other chiefs. I had to go to court and appear before a judge. I said to him that our

God Majikjiki, who appears on the new national flag of Vanuatu, is seen wearing nambas. You cannot stop me from following our native culture. I was supported by the government inspector (he never said from which department), who stopped the church from interfering with local kastom culture ever again, officially anyway. He told me that, if I was arrested by the police again, he would sack the officers. The island chiefs were delighted and I was set free.'

It is because of High Chief Wai Wai Rawi's courage that Vanuatu still has a kastom tradition. I was very proud of my brother. The Chief said that he was the most senior Chief on Tanna Island, as he alone holds the secret of the Kassoso.

'People from all over Tanna come to see me for counsel,' he said, 'to sort out their problems.'

The Chief smiled and looked at me, 'Iarueri, you were brought to me by Spirit to learn the truth. I tell you the secrets which must not be told to others.'

He then went on to tell me stories of the Kassoso, which I cannot disclose. The Chief stood and asked me to do some more healing with my magic stone. When I had done energy work with him before, I had used different techniques, including the use of a pendulum for dowsing energy blocks to be released. The Chief referred to the pendulum as my magic stone. The magic stone was something he could relate to in his culture and it was something tangible he could see and feel.

He led the way to Donald's village, where a group of people had obviously been waiting for some time for healing. The Chief called forward a young woman who held a crying baby. The woman's name was Kahibran. She had a hard lump the size of an egg on the left side of her neck. She handed her baby to Donald; the baby screamed. Everybody is family in the village; all seem to be related. Donald took the baby, wiping copious amounts of thick hanging yellow snot from her face, flicking it from his fingers on to the ground, then wiping his hand on his shorts. I looked into Kahibran's energy body and saw a black egg at the neck. I used my pendulum to connect with the appropriate aspect of her Higher Self to release the energetic counterpart, after getting the usual ethical permissions. I took her feet and massaged the reflexology pressure points for the throat and neck, both of which were painful. I showed her how to massage these points, as it is important to give people something to do.

The Chief said her baby cried day and night and wouldn't stop. Donald handed the baby back to her mother and she latched on to the breast to suckle. This quietened her temporarily, which allowed me to do some craniosacral therapy on the baby's head. She was very hot, looking at me tearfully, but refusing to hand back the nipple. After a few minutes, she calmed down and fell asleep. The Chief and others thought this most impressive (so did I!). The young mother stood slowly so not to disturb the sleeping infant and I was presented with another baby. This little boy was also very hot but would not allow me to hold his head gently, so I used the pendulum to do some surrogate dowsing for him via his mother.

The Chief then called forward Glenda. Glenda sat on the pandanus mat in the sun, looking a little embarrassed. The Chief gave me a command, 'Make her pregnant!'

Everybody crowded around. I wasn't sure what they thought I was going to do next so, to break the tension, I grabbed her feet. I gently massaged the reflex points to the ovaries, uterus and Fallopian tubes, and the pelvic area generally. The two points which caused her sharp pain were the left ovary and right Fallopian tube. This latter point was interesting, as she had a weeping tropical ulcer here. Flies drank thirstily at the oozing yellow pus.

I asked Glenda to lie down on the mat. She didn't speak or understand English so looked somewhat alarmed when she realised I wanted her to lie down. She pulled her dress tightly between her legs. I explained to the Chief what I was doing to do with my magic stone and he acted as interpreter. All the women started "clicking" with their tongues. I did some dowsing over her belly and at the same time scanned her energy body to see the state of her Vital Cauldron (see Appendix B). I saw clearly an image of a fresh wooden stake impaling her womb. I had learned this scanning technique from the Chief on my visit to Itabu in 2004. In essence, what this symbolised to me was a recent (fresh) psychic projection (wooden stake) from somebody who, for one reason or another, didn't want Glenda to become pregnant. It could have been a spell, curse or even self-sabotage. It really doesn't matter. What does matter is that when somebody asks for help and you get the relevant permission, you hand the situation over to Spirit to remove the intrusion in a safe, gentle and appropriate way, which is what happened.

A curse, in essence, is where an intrusive energy is consciously projected into another person's personal, sacred, sovereign space without permission. This includes misguided beliefs of sending love and healing to others when it is not requested. These attributes are different vibrational frequencies within universal consciousness. They are different levels of energy which, no matter how well intentioned, if projected into someone else's sacred space without permission, can have the effect of becoming curse-like. Sadly, many righteous religious people fall into this trap, which is ego based.

The magic stone began to swing wildly anti-clockwise over Glenda's belly, as the energetic intrusion was unwound and withdrawn, then gently circled clockwise as her own vitality and life force was returned to this area of her body. I indicated to Glenda that I had finished. The Chief offered his good hand to her to help her up. Glenda rubbed her belly and told the Chief she felt heat there, where before it felt cold. The Chief smiled at me. People whispered about Iarueri's magic stone. I have personally found in my shamanic practice that women who want children but cannot conceive or maintain early pregnancy, for whatever reason, have such a powerful heart's desire to nurture that they automatically draw to themselves lost, abandoned and frightened spirit children who are motherless and trapped between worlds. Maybe the role of these women is to love and care for these spirit children in this incarnation, not necessarily physical children. They are mothers.

The Chief called to Donald and told him to take me for a walk through the rain forest to show me some kastom places and to tell me stories. The Chief wanted me to see the place where hot coloured volcanic clay was obtained for painting their bodies for sacred ceremony.

We set off along the network of jungle trails, walking through a small village where we passed a middle-aged woman having a bath. She sat, fully clothed, in a muddy pool of water beneath the village stand pipe. A younger woman poured brown coloured water over her head from a yellow plastic bucket. It seems that women don't remove their clothing to wash in this culture.

We climbed up steeper paths until we were overlooking Itabu, now lost beneath the tree canopy. Donald said that where we were was Mt Namesas, known locally as the Eagle Roost. Donald explained that this is where the men collect the feathers from moulting eagles for ceremony. As if on cue, several eagles soared overhead. Donald pointed out two other nearby peaks, Mt Noqunessan and Mt Catcheba. The area was full of coconut palms, many felled from cyclonic winds. The forest floor was littered with coconuts, eaten by wild pigs and rats. Donald told me a kastom story about the rats, pointing to the neat holes cut into the fallen coconuts by these creatures.

'As the rats are native creatures, there is a spirit stone for them at another Chief's nakamal. This Chief contacted the rats and sent them to steal food from other people's gardens. One day, a certain man caught the King Rat and knocked out one of its teeth, putting a leaf in the empty socket, sending back the message that his garden was not to be raided again or there would be trouble. The King Rat returned to its nakamal and the Chief saw the leaf in its mouth, understanding its meaning. From that day on, the garden was never touched again.'

Rats are very intelligent creatures and have a vital role to play in nature in helping to control disease by consuming rotting corpses, meats, vegetables and fruits, most of which are discarded by humans.

Many years ago I lived in a farmhouse where, one day, a solitary hungry rat came to my front door looking for food early one winter. I promised the rat I would feed him and his kind every day throughout winter with the agreement that he would not come into my house, and I would not come into his, and that he had to leave in spring and not return. I kept my promise. He lived in a hole at the base of a stone wall in the garden and every morning I would put bread in his hole for him. By the time spring had arrived there were at least 12 rats which I fed daily. On the Spring Equinox, every rat disappeared and I never saw them ever again.

Donald explained that it was in this area that his grandfather stored copra (dried coconut flesh) for sale to Lenakel. This was the main export commodity of Vanuatu until recent times. 'We had to guard the coconut day and night with dogs to prevent the pigs from stealing it,' he said.

In the opening where the copra used to be dried, it was now abandoned to nature. Tall wild grasses grew and Boston ferns, known locally as sicciggy. Donald pointed to the ground and told me to put my hand on the earth. The ground was hot from the volcano. He cut some vines with his machete and showed me how to construct a wild chicken trap. He soon built a pyramid-like structure with woven cane sides to the apex, then bound together with strips of bark. A split peg was attached, under tension, to a fine piece of bark, which was triggered when the chicken knocked it with its leg, trying to reach the coconut bait inside. The door came down and the chicken was trapped. When the hunter came, he would bind the chicken by its feet. Donald explained that the same method was used to catch wild pussycats. They were good to eat, he said, then described what was done. 'You killed the cat, then cut off its tail to stop it smelling. You only ate the meat, not the head or guts. Cat meat makes you strong to lift heavy objects, to run or fight. Sometimes we would hunt the pussycat with dogs and kill it with a spear or with bow and arrow. Pussycat meat tastes sweet. The men in Lenakel eat rats and frogs. Dogs are eaten in neighbouring villages, but not here at Itabu. Horse meat is eaten near White Grass Airport and snakes are eaten in Port Vila.'

Donald shuddered and added that he was afraid of snakes. He picked up a coconut and cut it in two to give us some flesh to eat.

We journeyed on to the place where the clay was traditionally collected. The clay was hot to the touch and volcanic fumes gassed off nearby. The clay varied in colour from the different minerals of white, green, brown, red, yellow, blue and black. Donald collected small pieces of coloured clay, applying it on to his legs in sweeping finger patterns. The clay smelled sulphurous and pungent. Donald collected some for me, which he wrapped in leaves.

Donald beckoned me on. He explained about the different kastom plants we encountered, and their uses. We arrived at a large rock formation covered in thick hanging moss. The rock formation was smooth volcanic lava, obviously where it had flowed down the slopes and set after an eruption. A ledge protruded halfway down where a depression had formed, which was now full of fresh water seeping out of the rock face. Water dripped constantly from the moss, which was rich in mineral salts. Butterflies, hornets, bees, insects, birds and other forest creatures came to drink. I had been here before in 2004 on my journey to Mt Horredy to visit the place of origin of the tribal creation myth. This is where the tribe came to collect their drinking and washing water before the installation of a water tank and stand pipes in 2005. Discarded plastic buckets, bottles and litter were left since that time, which saddened me, as this was truly a magical place. Traditionally, all sacred places have a spirit guardian. I asked Donald the name of the guardian of this special place. He replied, 'He is known as Watnecremer.'

'My brother,' I replied, 'what do you think Watnecremer thinks of all of this rubbish left here in this sacred kastom place?'

Donald looked at me thoughtfully for a moment and replied that it should be removed. I smiled at him and encouraged him to organise this to be done.

Traditionally, tribal peoples have always consumed organic natural foods and built their homes from nature. It was natural to discard food and building debris on the land, at waterholes, along river banks or long paths or trails, as these items broke down naturally and returned back to the earth. With this habit strongly programmed within their psyche, when plastic, glass and cans were introduced into their environment and culture, they naturally discarded these items in nature as they had done for countless generations. Consequently, many pristine native lands are strewn with the rubbish and decay that causes pollution from the sickness of Western society.

We returned to Itabu, passing a thicket of tall mature bamboo. Donald used the back of his machete to hit different sized poles. This had the amazing effect of creating different sounds, depending on the amount of inner water held inside the cavities and size of the bamboo. It sounded like he was playing a crude form of xylophone.

Cooking pig over the Itabu nakamal fire.

We arrived back at the village. Donald's eldest son, Niai Paian, soon arrived carrying a package which he handed to his father. Donald smiled and opened the carefully wrapped leaves to reveal a large piece of wild honeycomb, oozing fresh honey. Donald offered me a large portion; it was delicious. He explained that the men had found a wild bees nest high in a palm tree, so they cut the tree down and smoked out the bees. I felt sad about this destruction, but this is what tribal life is about, basically survival.

I was told to rest after lunch and connect to Kassoso. Around dusk, Donald called for me to go to the nakamal. He gave me some kava roots to carry and he went to cut a short club to kill a pig.

On arrival at the nakamal, two strangers were talking to the Chief. Both were well-dressed, wearing shoes and socks and had clean shirts. This was very unusual. They smelled like Christian proselytes. I put my guard up as, when these people turned up, there was usually some trickery or deceit involved. All of the gathered kastom men sat huddled in a group well away from these two. I sat near to the Chief. He asked me to shake their hands and say hello, which I did. The kastom men glared at them. One of the Christians stood behind the Chief, the other leaned over and held his hand with a bowed head. The man standing behind the Chief started praying aloud with evangelical fervour, thanking Jesus for the miracle of healing. As they left, the kastom men spat on the ground in unison and the Christian in charge shouted, 'God bless you.'

I shouted back, 'And you, brothers!'

They laughed, then left. I didn't enquire as to which Christian cult they belonged.

A small, sapphire blue butterfly flitted past my face as I sat by the fire. I was then called to help prepare the kava. I was given some coconut fibre from the outer husk to scrub the soil off the kava roots. Donald killed a small pig to enable us to connect with Kassoso and it was butchered at the edge of the nakamal.

Again the kava was made strong for the Chief's benefit to aid his pain. The pig flesh was skewered on to pointed sticks, stuck in the ground at 45 degree angles. They were turned occasionally, when the fat burst into flames. After the kava, I was given two pieces of scorched lung, which was rubbery and still contained large raw blood clots, which burst in my fingers, covering my hands in congealed blood. The lung felt like large bloody slugs in my mouth. As I bit into a second portion of lung, a large blood clot exploded in my mouth, cascading outwards into my beard. The taste of raw blood wouldn't go away, so I prayed that I would be offered a second shell of kava to wash it down. As it happened, I was given some rice on a leaf plate, followed by some burnt meat.

I returned to the restaurant for my dinner to the sounds of the cicadas, singing in unison like massed choirs. Flying foxes wheeled overhead, foraging for fruit. No matter how often I washed my beard in soapy water, I could smell the blood on my face all night.

Part 2
The Awakening

Kassoso Fire   Healing   Kassoso Hand

Last night we had torrential rain. For the second night running, I heard a cat wailing around my hut. My chest had become worse and I had a sore throat and a hacking cough, which kept me awake for most of the night. The heavy rain seemed to ease by dawn. There was a leak in the roof of my hut, but fortunately not over the bed like it was the last time. The tam tam drum was played early in the morning for some reason. I never found out why. Because all of the windows in my leaf hut were open to the elements, the rain and damp air through the night had blown into the hut, so all of my clothes and bedding were wet.

By 7.30, the sun was out. It was hot, humid and sticky. Rivulets of sweat ran down my back. It was clear why locals wore the minimum of clothing. When you wear clothes, bacteria form and you smell; not so if naked.

Paths had been eroded away during the night with the heavy rain, washing away copious quantities of soil and silt to expose the bare rough volcanic rock beneath. Mynah birds bathed in the pools of water left in these stony places. Sulphur yellow butterflies flitted amongst the scarlet hibiscus flowers and yellow orchids. Green and red parakeets flew across the tree canopies, calling noisily to each other, as Yasur exploded in the near distance. Small black martins with white rumps chased insects through the palm fronds. Raindrops hung from the tree fronds and white lilies, like glistening jewels sparkling in the new morning sun. I was fascinated by the multitude of tropical plants and flowers, some of which I recognised from the tropical greenhouses when I was at horticultural college.

The Chief called briefly, when I was having breakfast, to say that he was going to the local market to buy some bananas for me. He would be straight back for more questions and answers he said. Knowing the Chief, this could be two hours or more later!

I went for a cold shower. The floor was covered with a thick layer of silt from the rains last night, which had blocked the small drain hole in the cement base of the shower. After washing, I filled my water bottle from the communal stand pipe, noticing a large black earwig-like insect, which was flushed out of the tap nozzle into my bottle. I put him safely in the bushes.

The Chief returned about an hour later. He asked me if I had dreamt about Kassoso. I said I hadn't. He went on to tell me of his dream where Kassoso said to him that we were not allowed to touch their bodies, but only their sticks. The Chief said that their stick was black, about three feet long, pointed at both ends. He also dreamt about his father, who said I was ready now to touch the Kassoso stick to receive

Toilet and shower hut – reserved for guests.

their power. The Chief continued explaining that it was the Kassoso who created fire. 'When you die, you leave your body here and your spirit returns along the road to the fire in Yasur volcano, from where it came. You get a new body and join the ranks of Kassoso.'

The Chief emphasised that everybody in the world comes to Yasur when they die, to be transformed and purified in the sacred fires. 'This is why Yasur means "Old Man". It is another name for God. When I die, there will be three days of cutting coconuts; then I will be buried. Donald has to kill a pig and take kava to open the road for me to the volcano and Kassoso, for my spirit to go into the fire. Donald must say these words for me: "The road for you is good. It is time for you to go down the hole into the volcano." When I die, I can talk to you; when you die, you can talk to me. I am very happy for our connection together. Iarueri, the people in the West can make matches, ships and aeroplanes, but they cannot connect to Kassoso. This is our gift from God.'

I asked the Chief if he had heard any more news about the police proceedings against the driver who caused the accident. The Chief replied that his medical costs were about 50,000 Vatu (approximately £400 in today's conversion rates), which could be ongoing in the future. As it was the other driver's fault, he has to pay the

Chief's medical expenses, plus damage to the hired truck, plus a fine or go to prison. This is a huge amount for a local person to find and pay.

The Chief said ruefully, 'In the olden days, he would have been eaten!'

I laughed. On my last visit to Itabu, the Chief had allowed the local Seventh Day Adventist Christians to start building a church at the roadside, much to my dismay, knowing how deceitful they were. I asked him why he had allowed this and he said that he had to provide for all of his people. I remember asking him what he would do if they started taking over the land and trying to convert the kastom people against their will. He replied that he would stop them. The church is still at the same stage of partial build as it was two years ago, so I asked him why it hadn't been completed.

He replied, 'Because all of the local kastom people came to me objecting about it and the Christians tried to take the land off me.' The Chief said, 'I told them to leave and build their church at White Sands near the airport.' (That was far enough away, I mused.)

The Chief got up to leave, telling me to connect to Kassoso. I returned to my hut and went into meditation. I found myself at the nakamal. The red pig with the golden tusks came out of the banyan tree to greet me. The pig went to the centre of the nakamal and started to scratch at the ground with its front hoof, causing a pool of blood to form, which became bigger until it was about four feet across. Then, suddenly, it burst into flames where a Kassoso emerged from the earth, all black with the body of a human and the head of a flying fox. In its right hand, it held a staff, which was a smooth black stick, pointed at both ends. This being grew until it became giant-like. I felt myself growing in equal stature alongside of it. Then, when we were both about 20 feet high, it turned its face to look at me, still consumed in flames, thrusting its staff towards me, which became a rod of fire. For some reason, my arm was heavy and I couldn't move it, even though I knew that I must touch the rod. Eventually, I managed to take hold of the staff, feeling my fingers curl around the flaming shaft. I felt a physical pressure behind my eyes and a sensation of being turned inside out. I began to sink to my knees, releasing my hold on the flaming rod. As soon as I had done this, Kassoso returned back into the earth, leaving the pool of blood. I became normal human size again. The red pig then put its snout to the edge of the pool of blood and it too returned back into the earth.

The Chief called me for lunch. It was fish from the local market; it was not cooked properly and still contained the entrails. I ate a little to be polite; it didn't taste good.

Donald and I were sent off up the mountains to Sergay village for me to do some healing on Chief Kabari. On the way through the jungle trails, we passed manioc, kava, pawpaw, banana, coconut and island cabbage growing in gardens. At one point, we had to negotiate a deep ditch by walking across a notched log. We duly arrived at Sergay nakamal. The first person I was told to work with was a young woman who had liver problems. I scanned her body and saw a black spike in her liver, which Spirit removed for her.

People started to gather and Chief Kabari arrived. He had chest problems, he said, and had difficulty in breathing, so I scanned his energy body and saw a stone-like object crushing his chest. I asked Spirit for this to be removed, which it was. There was a pause after the Chief's healing as people started to gather and talk. I watched a young boy hunting small birds with a catapult amongst the big banyan trees. Then another young man arrived; his name was Nigkow. He was the son of Chief Kabari. He asked me to do more work on Kahibran, his wife. The lump in her neck didn't bother her so much now, he said, and her baby didn't cry any longer. When I worked with her, the black egg I saw yesterday in her energy body had become soft and more pliable, easier to release. Spirit was able to remove it now.

I was asked then to work on an old lady who was blind in one eye, who had a fever and back problems. Again, I scanned her energy body and saw a wooden splinter in the occiput region on the right-hand side of her head. Then I was asked to treat Nigkow's son, who had the exact same neck problem as his mother. I did reflexology on all who attended as well.

I remembered this village from a previous visit when it was called Ianakun. I was confused by the name change, recalling memories I had, which the villagers were pleased about. The day was very hot and humid; my clothes were saturated with sweat. I knew that I smelled, yet the consolation was that everybody did! Our exchange payment was some manioc, so we returned to Itabu, and, after a brief rest, went to the nakamal.

The Chief was already there and had wrapped around his hand a clean shirt bandage. He unwrapped the bandage to reveal that the cut which the kastom doctor had made had been given five stitches at the hospital and also the ends of his fingers where the bones had been protruding. The kastom doctor wanted to split the back of the hand to release the swelling and the bad blood, but the Chief refused, saying that he had had enough.

I noticed for the first time this evening that the volcanic vents around the sides of the nakamal were smoking, which had not been apparent before. Young boys had

Boys with their "cars".

constructed "cars" by building a long pole with a wooden crossbar as handles at the top and a crossbar at the bottom that hinged on a nail. At the ends of the lower crossbar were nailed tuna cans on either side that acted as wheels. The top end of the pole rested over the boy's shoulder as they pushed the device along in front of them. Every village I saw, the local boys had built these cars.

After participating in the kava ritual, I returned to the restaurant for my evening meal and then back to my leaf hut to sleep. I prayed to Kassoso to connect with me, to bring to me their grace and knowledge, to help me to understand the unique connection between them and the High Chief lineage.

At about 11.40 pm, I was suddenly woken by something tugging sharply at my sheets. It was pitch black, so I scrabbled in the darkness to find my torch, shining it initially at my alarm clock, then the bed. An arm reached in through the open window from outside, pulling sharply at my bedding. Initially, I felt afraid that it was an intruder trying to hurt me or break in. I tried to work out who was the nearest person to me in the village if I needed urgent help, realising it would be Nahu who was about 500 yards away. I didn't know what to do, so I instinctively grabbed the hand and held it firmly. My mind cleared sufficiently to wonder if it were the Kassoso. I shouted, 'Hello, hello.' The arm pulled away into the darkness outside. I shone my torch through the window. There was nobody there!

Then the arm came back through the window again, so I reached up under the curtain, holding the hand firmly. It felt coarse and rough, like a labourer's calloused hand. As I held the hand with one of mine, I shone the torch through the window with my other hand. There was no body there. This freaked me out somewhat! I felt the hand close its fingers tightly around mine and saw the arm reaching through the window, but there was no body attached to the other end of the arm. I instinctively closed my hand more tightly around its. Whatever it was, it began to make snorting noises, then a sharp barking sound, 'Yeuh, Yeuh, Yeuh!'

It wasn't human. Suddenly, it let go of my hand and pulled away. I sat upright in the bed, staring into the darkness as I heard it walk slowly around the hut and try to open my door. The door was shaken and rattled, but it couldn't get in. I heard it leaving. There was total silence until a dog started to howl a few minutes later, like a baying wolf, continuously for 20 minutes. This didn't sound natural either. What was strange was that no other dog howled with it, as they normally did. The volcano exploded suddenly, which startled me, then the night fell eerily silent. I badly wanted to urinate, but no way was I going to venture out into the pitch black darkness, so I felt where the gaps in the floorboards were the widest in the corner of the hut and urinated through the floor. I felt afraid. Was someone trying to frighten me for some reason or was it really my first physical encounter with Kassoso? I prayed to Kassoso not to hurt me or those who I loved, explaining who I was and why I had come to their land.

9th October 2012
Grandfather Iarueri in Prison   Tokka

It rained heavily through the night. I felt restless after the encounter with the mystery hand. My alarm went off at 5 am, as we were going to the Tokka Festival today. The Chief had organised two trucks for an early 6 am departure. I felt exhausted. By 5.30 am, I was drenched in sweat due to the still air and the high humidity. My clothes and bedding were wet, as they couldn't dry out. The easiest way, of course, to dry wet clothes is to wear them. This time of year was the beginning of the rainy season, so therefore the mosquito season. Where there was standing water, mosquitoes were already breeding, especially in the thousands of broken coconut shells which littered the forest floor, containing considerable amounts of rain water. The streams and rivers would soon start to flow in spate.

The Chief had also organised an early breakfast for me – tea and dog biscuits. On the way to the restaurant, I rescued a large brown and cream coloured jungle snail, which was about four inches long, crossing the path,. I put it in the bushes for safety, as the children tend to mistreat these creatures. The Chief arrived early, as I was having my breakfast. I told him what happened during the night. He was bent over double for long enough, laughing, tears running down his face. 'Kassoso, Iaureri, Kassoso!' he exclaimed. 'They have changed the rules again now they have touched you. We did ceremony last night at the nakamal to Tamaffa to open the road for you to touch them. It has begun.'

I told the Chief about the dog howling. He said that this was not Kassoso making that sound, but the dog must have seen Kassoso passing by and was afraid. I asked the Chief what I should do if it happened again. He laughed in his usual manner and told me to hold their hand gently, not roughly. The Chief automatically went into story telling mode as we waited for our transport to arrive.

'The church tried to stop the Tokka Festival. The Presbyterian Church was the worst, as the two colonial powers, Britain and France, supported their actions. My grandfather, Iarueri, and other kastom men from Itabu were arrested and put in prison in Lenakel, then transferred to a prison in Port Vila. He was in prison for a year. The police made a big fire and forced Iarueri and the other prisoners to run through the flames as punishment. Many suffered severe burns, which became infected. They received no food for a month, but were forced to drink salt water which made them sick. After a month, they were given a small amount of rice to eat.

'They were kept in prison until the Second World War, when Japan invaded the Solomon Islands. The Americans came and they forced the police to release the prisoners. Iarueri persuaded the Americans to get the kastom culture reinstated by the then government of the New Hebrides, now Vanuatu. Iarueri told the authorities that they had no right to stop their ancient culture and they couldn't stop him and the others from following their traditions. As the Americans had helped the kastom people, some local folk adopted the American flag as a symbol of freedom and the John Frum Cult was born. Some of the kastom men in prison died, five that I knew of, some in Lenakel, others in Port Vila. The prisons held 100 men. All of the prisoners had their clothes taken, so they were naked. Once the Americans came, the kastom people could start their circumcision rituals and ceremonies again without persecution.

'After Iarueri's release, he returned to Itabu, but he was very sick. The kastom men had no power to resist the police who had guns. The police beat some prisoners to death. In Tanna, the authorities brought in other black men from different tribes and islands to control us. Grandfather Iarueri was dying, so he was carried on a stretcher up into a remote village in the mountains, where he died and where he is now buried in their nakamal. When grandmother Natu died, she was buried near to him.

'My father is buried in the Itabu nakamal and that is where I will be buried. Only Chiefs are permitted to be buried in the nakamal. Mitac (the Chief's wife who died in 2008) is buried in Donald's encampment outside the nakamal. Ordinary people are buried wherever they want in the forest. My great-grandfather Rawi is also buried in the nakamal at Itabu. We keep our ancestors' stories in our heads. When Donald dies, then the next High Chief will be Donald's firstborn son, Niai Paian, not Jack (the Chief's second born son).

'Tanna has black stone from the volcano. There are two types – light and heavy. We have no trouble digging graves here. In Santo, they have white stone that needs to be broken with a crowbar to dig a grave. These graves are shallow, so pigs can dig up the corpses to eat them in certain places.'

A truck arrived at 7.30 am. I was instructed to pack a small bag with what I needed, as we were staying for a couple of nights, along with thousands of other people. As we waited for the second truck to arrive, I looked in fascination at the utter beauty of nature around me. The majority of orchids were beginning to come into flower bud, trees were festooned with these magnificent plants. Seedlings were bursting through the rich volcanic earth just waiting for the opportunity to show the world their innate magnificence, beauty and potential.

By 8.30, there was still no sign of the second truck, which clearly frustrated the Chief. He decided to leave. So much for an early start! You have to be very flexible with the kastom way of life, no schedules or plans are adhered to. This is called living in the moment!

People scrambled to get into the back of the truck. I was invited to sit in the rear seat of the cab, along with Nahu and a child. The driver stopped at Iaqurimano village, where we waited for another driver to take us to the village where the Tokka Festival was being held. After some time, a man who looked familiar arrived and I recognised it was Moses, my guide and interpreter from my stay in 2004. Moses used to be a taxi driver in Port Vila, so he was an experienced driver.

When we passed the volcanic ash plain, we had to ford a river in four-wheel drive to climb up the bank at the far side. The riverbed had been dry on my arrival but was becoming more swollen by the heavy tropical rains. On the way to Lenakel, we stopped countless times when either Moses or the Chief wanted to talk to different

Traditional tree fern carving in Itabu village, just under 5 metres high, representing the ancestors.

people. Once we had passed over Snake Hill and dropped down from the mountain range, the weather changed dramatically to be very hot, sunny and dry. I was fascinated at the variety of different forms of plants and flowers that grew in this environment, quite different to Itabu. Especially what I found fascinating was the "morning glory", a type of convolvulus which cascaded from trees in thick carpets of deep blue flowers. Huge white, cream, yellow and pink trumpet-like flowers hung in profusion of brugmansia, often called datura or "angel's trumpets", a highly poisonous shrub of the potato family, Solanaceae.

We passed gangs of construction workers labouring on the new highway. Large bulldozers were smashing down trees and pushing them to one side. Some locals carried off the wood, presumably for their fires. The destruction was sickening. What would the ancestors and Spirit do, I wondered.

We arrived at Lenakel at 10 am. The Chief wanted to buy bread and other food for our stay at Yapenawan village, hosting the Tokka Festival. After getting some supplies, we headed south-west towards the coast, meeting Nikwei walking along a dry dusty road leading out of the town. We were delighted to see each other again. I was saddened that he had had to leave Itabu under pressure to be with his family in Lenakel, as he clearly wasn't happy. He was a good friend. I had brought with me a smoking pipe and tobacco, just in case of this very opportunity of meeting up with him again. He was delighted with these gifts. We pressed on, leaving Nikwei standing in a cloud of dust, waving.

We soon reached the coast, driving along rough dirt roads, which followed the black coastal sands and reefs. Large breakers broke against the shore, yet the beaches were empty of people. The deep blue Pacific Ocean reached endlessly to the far horizon without a ship in sight. It felt timeless. We came to a junction in the road veering off from the coastal track into the bush, climbing in four-wheel drive into another mountain range.

We arrived at Yapenawan village. There was a traffic jam, as many other vehicles were arriving or leaving. After parking the truck, Moses, the Chief and I wandered around. A totally new village around the perimeter of the original village had been constructed to house and feed the dancers and spectators. It was just like a refugee camp. There were dormitory-like sleeping quarters, restaurants, kitchens, butchers, pig pens, shops and latrines. Dancing was already underway, four different groups of women competing in the napen-napen dance. They were all beautifully attired in coloured grass skirts, tinsel, plastic flowers, feather sticks and colourful tops. All had their faces painted. The Chief was unimpressed and shook his head sadly with dismay at the lack of kastom etiquette.

The women's
napen-napen
dance

The organisers had estimated that 1,000 people were already present; many more were expected later. People had been preparing for this festival for four years and many had walked all night from different parts of Tanna Island to participate or to be a spectator. Some had travelled from other islands. I saw a couple of old women in plain grass skirts, who were barebreasted, without face paint or ornamentation. This was the true kastom way. A few minutes later, I noticed at the perimeter a couple of very old men, who were naked, except for nambas. I was delighted that I had witnessed at least four people honouring the old ways.

Tokka originally would have brought warring tribes together to settle their differences, each group competing with their own dances. All would then dance together and all the pigs and food brought would have been killed and eaten for a feast. This would also be a time for marriages to be arranged and trading to take place. Those who had grievances could seek counsel from the Chiefs and Elders.

I was told that the Tokka would go on for the following two days and nights, when more people would gather and camp, until the finale on the third morning for the actual Tokka Dance at dawn. After the dance, 400 pigs would be slaughtered. The first two days, the women dance and their menfolk have to look after the children to enable the women to take the time off from their difficult hard-working lives. Every principal woman dancer has to supply a pig, and these are gifts for the male dancers. The male dancers also have to bring a pig each, and these are gifts for the women dancers.

I needed to urinate so asked the Chief where the toilet was. He directed me to one of the many latrines dug especially for the festival. This particular latrine had a deep wide pit dug into the ground, which was screened off by woven palm leaves. Across the pit were placed large logs with a strategically placed hole in the centre. As usual, men had not aimed well, so the logs were slippery with urine, which the flies found attractive. There was a surprising amount of excrement already in the pit, with lots of green leaves, which the local people use as their toilet "paper".

The Chief and I were hungry, as we had had an early breakfast, so he decided to go to a restaurant to have a meal. We were given a plate each of boiled rice and one chicken wing. We returned to the nakamal to enjoy the spectacle of the massed dancers charging across the ground, covering everybody with choking dust. It was very powerful. Hundreds of spectators roared with excitement to the drumming and chanting of these women, who were clearly in warrior mode.

Massed dancers

Carrying the Chief and Yeramanu.

Suddenly, there was an excited commotion as the crowd parted for the arrival of the Chief and Yeramanu who were hosting this event. A party of about 20 men bore a large bamboo platform on poles across their shoulders, which carried the Chief and Yeramanu in full tribal dress. They waved to the crowd as they entered the "arena" and were carried around a considerable distance to do a lap of honour. Between both men were roots of the sacred tabunga kava, which would be prepared and drunk by the Chief and Elders after the Tokka Dance itself on the last day.

The women sang kastom songs in different tribal languages, beating woven pads containing leaves. When several hundred of these pads are beaten, it sounds like a gathering of massed drums. All dances told stories about kastom life, myth and legend. The dancers were goaded by young men, threatening them with short pointed sticks; they shouted and danced to try to put the women off their songs and routine. This was their official role in the napen-napen. All of a sudden, the women would charge the boys, sending them into the crowd, screaming and laughing, kicking up thick yellow dust, which caused the dancers to disappear briefly. The women would then throw sweets or tobacco braids into the group of boys. This went on for most of the day. In essence, the boys acted as the jesters, the tricksters. Other men, with clubs and sticks, moved around the perimeter of the dancing women, to keep the crowds back. If anyone tried to touch one of the women or interfere with the dance, these men would attack them. The Chief said that, occasionally, people did get killed.

At about 4 pm, the dancers changed over to allow those who had been performing all day to return home to prepare and cook for tomorrow. The Chief decided not to stay as planned, returning to Lenakel hospital to have his hand looked at, as he was still in considerable pain. Moses parked in an area of the hospital with a sign that clearly said "No Parking", which was right outside the hospital mortuary. The mortuary door, hanging on broken hinges, was wide open. The hospital was very basic. The Chief had his fingers redressed and was told to return in two days for the stitches to be removed.

We did some more food shopping in Lenakel after picking up Nikwei, who wanted to drink kava with me at Itabu. We stopped at Lamanebibi village at White Sands to see Enoch, the Chief's youngest son and to give him some vegetables which the Chief bought at a roadside stall.

When we returned to Itabu, we went directly to the nakamal. Once again, the perennial problem of the church versus kastom culture was brought up by the men. They asked me about Jesus; was he a real person? I said that, in the West, he is often portrayed as a white man with fair hair and blue eyes, but, if you believe there was such a person and the story was true, then it is logical that, if he lived in the desert, he would have been a dark-skinned man with black hair and brown eyes. The men fell about laughing at this statement.

Nikwei had an impressive beard now, mostly white. I asked the Chief why he had shaved his beard off and he said that it was kastom tradition to shave it off if you were sick. It would grow again now. Nikwei put a maize cob in the fire to roast for me as an exchange for his pipe. It was delicious. The Chief told me to leave my hut door open for the Kassoso tonight. The Chief said that no strangers would come into the village during the night, as his dogs would "get them". I left the nakamal and went for my dinner.

During the night, I began to feel nauseous and unable to sleep. I heard a strange sharp tapping sound from inside the leaf hut in the middle of the night; at the same time, the flying foxes were screaming overhead. By morning, I had diarrhoea and severe belly cramps and had to go to the toilet several times. I was concerned that I would not be well enough to return to the festival.

10th October 2013
Sickness   Tokka Latrines

I woke at dawn, feeling very ill. I went to the restaurant at 7 o'clock, refusing breakfast, which was a pity as it was bread and fresh fruit. All I could stomach was hot water. The Chief and Donald arrived. I was asked if I had dreamt about Kassoso.

I told them that I didn't dream but I had heard a strange tapping sound in the middle of the night inside my hut. As it was pitch black, I couldn't see anything. The Chief laughed and Donald smiled broadly.

'That was Kassoso, Iarueri,' the Chief exclaimed. 'They were inside your hut, looking at you in bed, tapping their stick to let them know they were with you.'

I thought to myself: typical, why can't the Kassoso come up to me at dusk or dawn and say 'Hello, Iarueri. We are Kassoso and have come to bring you sacred knowledge and to reconnect you back to the first ancestors,' then offering their hand to me to shake in brotherhood and friendship!

Connecting to Spirit or interdimensional shapeshifting beings is hard work if you have no "yardstick" from which to work. Equally, the Chief never tells me too much at once, just a snippet here and there to keep me hanging by a thread. "Is this another test for me," I wondered, "to see how determined and dedicated I am?"

The Chief's hand had reduced in swelling and looked a lot better now. The Chief changed the subject, asking me how I was. I explained that I felt sick, with a fever, nausea and diarrhoea. I told him that I was unsure if I would be well enough to go to the Tokka, as I needed to run to the toilet every few minutes. He looked sad, 'Rest, Iarueri, we will see how you are this afternoon. Connect to Kassoso.'

I returned to my hut and immediately vomited at the base of a hibiscus shrub. I hoped it would be grateful for a little pre-digested organic fertiliser. I felt much better afterwards, although I was still burning up with fever. I slept well for a couple of hours, which is what I needed. There was a light tapping at the door. The Chief called to me to see how I was. He was clearly concerned for my welfare. He wanted to know if I wanted anything to eat and if I was able to go to Tokka. I asked for some bread for the journey, as I hadn't had to run to the toilet for a couple of hours. I hoped the sickness was passing now.

All of my clothes were wet because of the constant rain and some leather items were mildewed. All of my recently handwashed laundry was still hanging in my hut, wringing wet. By midday, the heavy rain had stopped and the sun came out; everything started to steam dramatically. A light breeze got up, so I put my wet laundry on the clothes line outside and washed everything else I could, so I knew I would have clean clothes on my return from the Tokka Festival.

The truck arrived at 2 pm. Sam was our driver, a young man with closely cropped hair, slightly balding with a trimmed black beard. He had a pleasant, open face and appeared to be very gentle in nature. We all duly piled into the truck, with a five-seater cab. The back of the truck had planks for those outside to sit on, luggage and provisions stacked in the centre. Again, I was invited to take a seat inside the cab. Sam and the Chief were in the front; Nahu, a small boy and I were in the back, as before. Donald stayed at Itabu as he wanted to finish planting his taro crop. Normally, the Ni-vans (short for Ni-Vanuatu, meaning "of our land", as Vanuatu generally means "our land") body odour does not bother me, but today, as I was still feeling ill, their body odour, combined with the coconut oil they used in the confines of the airless truck, made me feel nauseous in the heat. I kept my face to the open window to get some fresh air.

Sam was a slow nervous driver, whereas Moses drove fast, with competence. Sam sat on the edge of his seat the entire journey to Lenakel and took over half an hour longer to get there than Moses. The Chief told Nahu to give me some bread to eat. Nahu hauled a sandwich from a plastic bag which she had made before breakfast, containing "nature identical strawberry jam", tomato and lettuce. Normally, this gourmet feast would have been warmly received, but all I wanted was plain bread. I picked at the bread, returning the sandwich to Nahu who shared it with everyone else.

We stopped at Lenakel, at the market near the beach, to buy more fresh bread for tonight's meal. As Nahu and others went shopping for food, I stood by the truck enjoying the sunshine, watching boys in shorts diving off the wharf into the sea. On the other side of the beach were women and girls, who gracefully glided into the water, fully clothed, from the black reefs.

We eventually arrived at Yapenawan village but had to park the truck some distance from the nakamal, as we were late arriving. By the time we had made our way to the village, it was dark. Since yesterday, the village had grown, with more makeshift huts, tents and wooden frames, which had blue tarpaulins tied over them. People were putting their bedding in the sleeping huts or rolling out their mats and blankets on the open ground on any spot that was vacant. In some shelters, there were over 20 people sleeping side by side.

I felt the urge to go to the toilet, glad that I had had the forethought to bring plenty of toilet paper with me, which was jammed in all of my pockets for such an event. The organisers had erected temporary lighting, powered by a petrol generator. The lights threw eerie shadows around the village. Dancing continued through the night, as usual. The Chief said that, in the olden days, they would light several fires to give heat and light. It often got chilly at night near the coast. I asked the Chief where the nearest toilet was, so he asked someone nearby, who directed us to the edge of the village to a group of trees. Again, this latrine was fenced off with woven palm leaf screens. I negotiated the slippery logs over the deep pit without any problems. The Chief shouted to me, reaching around the corner with a handful of leaves. As I was about to leave, my curiosity got the better of me unfortunately. I shone my head torch into the pit. That was a bad mistake. I was surprised at the wide spectrum of colour of human excrement – greys, browns, reds, yellows, greens, olives and blacks. There was a seething mass of maggots, performing their dance, and cockroaches sat together, enjoying their picnic. Of course, there were no handwashing facilities, so I used some hand sanitiser which Maggie had given to me for such occasions.

The Chief was waiting for me at the latrine entrance. We picked our way through the darkness to where our little party waited and sat. To my utter dismay, I realised I had trodden in human shit which, on inspection in torch light, revealed that the cleats of my right boot were thick with green excrement. The smell was horrendous. I don't know what its previous owner had had to eat the day before, but it was very rancid. Nahu and the others moved away from me. I started to rub my boot onto the roots of a nearby tree and into the earth to rid myself of this filth as best I could. The Chief shouted to me, 'Dance, Iarueri, dance!'

The others fell about laughing. I felt mortified and embarrassed. This reminded me of the time Maggie and I were in Madagascar. We were staying at a place on the southern coast for a few days. I had decided to get up at dawn to go for a walk along the beach. Above the high water mark was nothing more than a human toilet for that part of town. Where the sea washed the sands was the only safe place to walk so, on my return, I carefully picked my way through the sand to the road a few yards away. To my horror, I had stood in a fresh pile of loose excrement, which had been sprinkled with fine sand to camouflage it. The camouflage worked really well! I returned to our hotel room, where I spent the next 20 minutes poking out the shit from the boot cleats with a sharp stick. I then struck a major problem. The previous owner had obviously been chewing pink chewing gum, which he (I didn't know why I felt male, but somehow it didn't feel female) had swallowed and had passed through his digestive system intact. It was well and truly stuck to my boot and I couldn't get it off! The combination of the sweet and sour smells was nauseating. It took three days of bush walking to finally clean my boot.

We ate some bread, which I enjoyed. I chatted to a few tourists who had come to see the Tokka. One of the organisers approached the Chief and spoke with him; then he approached us and said that all of the Westerners had to have their faces painted because, if you wandered outside the perimeter by mistake during the night, the guards would kill you, which would be a problem. I think he took his responsibilities to extremes! Three red stripes were daubed across my forehead. This was to stop gatecrashers, we were told. I thought it more likely a local would try to creep in rather than a tourist!

The Chief and I left the rest of the group and climbed up a rickety bamboo ladder, which had a guard posted at its base, to an equally rickety scaffold of bamboo and timber. That was one of the newly constructed viewing platforms for those who paid a little extra. The platform could hold about 20 people. Every time someone walked across it, it swayed and creaked. We heard a similar bamboo platform on the opposite side of the nakamal crack and split as it gave way. People shouted, but nobody was hurt.

Dancing had been going on all day and continued all night. It was truly spectacular and very powerful to have 1,000 dancers charging down one side of the nakamal, shouting and beating drum pads, then up the other side, covering everybody in a thick coating of fine yellow dust, kicked up by thrashing heels. There were no mosquitoes and the evening was pleasantly mild. We stayed up on the platform all night.

A thousand dancers charge across the nakamal.

The men's dawn Tokka dance, also known as the Nekowiar ceremony at Yapenawan.

A thousand male dancers gathered, some holding staffs, who began a dance with a deep chanting rhythm rather like a war cry. At certain points within the dance, the men, in full tribal regalia, charged to the opposite side of the nakamal as if they were a massed army going for the attack against their enemy. This charge and chant sequence lasted for several minutes until 1,000 dancers had totally disappeared in thick yellow dust. Spectators ran in confusion in all directions as the warriors wielded their staffs into the crowd. The intense energy was breathtaking. At each charge the men seemed to draw upon more stamina until they were acting like a group of wheeling starlings, seemingly following group mind consciousness. People shouted and danced in the spectator areas as everyone became delirious with collective raw energy. It was one of the most amazing spectacles I have ever witnessed.

11th October 2013:
Tokka Dance   Sick Woman   Restaurant

By 4.30 am, the different dances had been completed. Throughout the three days and nights, "stewards" patrolled the dancers and the dancing area, culling out fallen headdresses, feather sticks, tinsel, plastic flowers and pieces of grass skirting with their long sticks to keep the dancing space clear of debris. Dawn was beginning to break. It was time for the Tokka Dance, the principal dance of the festival.

The Chief strained his eyes in the darkness, searching for the procession of dancers. He spotted the men approaching, pointing excitedly. Out from under the big banyan trees walked a massed crowd of male dancers, who carried a huge pole, about 15 feet tall and phallic-like, covered completely in chicken feathers. At the top were long, curved, black and white rooster tail feathers and up the entire length of the shaft, bands of smaller feathers, alternating white, brown and black rings. This sacred pole was supported by the Tokka sticks of the dancers close enough to reach it (the Tokka stick is like a long-handled hockey stick).

When the dancing and singing started, it was truly amazing. The Chief, wide-eyed and laughing like a small child, was a spectacle in himself. Most of the men wore their tribal grade belts. The Tokka dancing, followed by fighting dances, continued uninterrupted until about 10 am. The Chief and I had spent about 15 hours on the swaying platform, watching continuously, fascinated at such a privileged opportunity of finally being a part, energetically anyway, of this festival, held exclusively on Tanna Island, where the original dance was birthed after a dream by one of the Chief's ancestors at Itabu.

The Chief didn't feel too well, so he wanted to leave early after the last dance, so we did not witness the ritual slaughter of the pigs. The last full Tokka Festival was

Carrying the sacred pole.

held at White Sands in 2004, as the one scheduled for 2008 was cancelled for some reason. If it all goes according to plan, the next Tokka Festival will be held in 2016. The Chief is considering the possibility of hosting it at Itabu village at that time.

We eventually rounded up the rest of our party and made our way back to our truck, where Sam was waiting. I learned that Sam's kastom name is Tunga Koata. His father is the Chief's brother, who has been given the role of Yeni, a similar role to a Yeramanu. I had so many questions I wanted to ask the Chief about what I had witnessed. I decided to wait until we had a chance to talk together without too many distractions.

As we were driving back to Lenakel, we had to take care because both sides of the dirt track were lined with pedestrians making their way home who were carrying small children and their camping gear. We rounded a bend and I happened to notice what appeared to be a pile of discarded rags under some shrubs about 20 feet from the roadside. As we passed, the Chief suddenly shouted for Sam to pull off the road and stop. Sam reversed back a few yards. The Chief jumped out of the truck and walked slowly to the pile of rags, which turned out to be a woman. The Chief shouted to her – no response. He bent over her head, shouting into her ear – still no response. The Chief glanced back to the truck, raising his eyebrows. We all knew what that meant – was she dead? The Chief began to shake her by the shoulder, shouting at her to try to get some response. She slowly opened her eyes and rolled over. She was clearly very sick and weak. The Chief called to those in the back of the truck to help him to get the girl into the vehicle. I offered to sit in the back so she could have my seat. The Chief refused, telling me to stay where I was. Many helping hands got the young woman into the back of the truck, where she was given the last of our bread to eat and water to drink. It appeared that she hadn't eaten for several days. After questioning her, the Chief decided to take her home to Lenakel, not to the hospital. Somebody in the truck had a cell phone, so word eventually got through to her family to meet her at a particular place in Lenakel. Her family were waiting for her as we arrived and helped her home.

The Chief wanted the two of us to go to a restaurant for a proper meal. Usually when we are in Lenakel, we used to go to a particular fish restaurant on the beach by the market place. The building had totally disappeared. He stopped a local woman and asked her where a restaurant was and was directed accordingly. Sam drove the truck up a particular street, where he parked. The Chief told everyone else to do what they wanted, as Iarueri and he were going for dinner! I felt somewhat embarrassed at this statement, enquiring if we should all go. The Chief simply said, 'No.'

The Chief got lost, so we were directed a second time down a narrow alley to a small establishment, which, on entering through a bead curtain to keep the flies out, was small but clean. Four small round tables were neatly laid out with cutlery and napkins, some paper, the others linen. The Chief went to the counter and ordered two meals, but had no idea what would come, as he couldn't read the menu. I prayed it wouldn't be lap lap (Vanuatu's national dish – a glutinous mass made from root crops cooked in an earth oven. It was like chewing geriatric slugs and virtually indigestible).

A counter separated the dining area from the kitchen, with a cloth hanging from the dividing door frame. When the wind blew open the cloth, you could see the cook chopping raw chicken on a piece of wood on the floor, then handling other foods without washing her hands. I expected another session of diarrhoea and vomiting, but equally realised that I had to build up my body's resistance to the local varieties of bacteria. I put my trust and faith in Spirit that I would be perfectly all right, as my mindset was that I was hungry and I was looking forward to my first proper meal in almost three days.

When our plates were brought to our table, I was delighted to see chicken wing, rice, tomato, lettuce, carrots and gravy. I thoroughly enjoyed the meal. What I left, the Chief finished. I had to pay for the meals, of course! Then we left.

I saw a new sign which said "Take Away" outside a shop near to the restaurant, seeing a woman emerging with a plastic bag containing several polystyrene containers of food. I felt sad as this was the first Take Away establishment in the town. Soon Lenakel and the wild places would be littered with another form of Western rubbish that will blow about in the wind and not rot away for many years, if at all.

We arrived back at Itabu at 2.30 pm. The Chief told me to have a shower to wash off the yellow dust that covered us all from the Tokka dancing, but there was no water available. I returned to my hut, brushing off as much dust from my hair and clothing as I could. My laundry was still wet, as Itabu had had constant heavy rain until today, we were told.

The Chief came to my hut, apologising that there was no kava left to drink in the nakamal tonight. He had sent two girls to the local market to buy some for tomorrow. He said that, by the time the girls returned with it, it would be too late to prepare for tonight. 'We will do kava tomorrow properly, to connect with Kassoso. I will come for you later so we can talk around the fire at the nakamal.'

As the Chief left, I could hear him singing the Tokka songs far off into the distance.

At 4 pm, the Chief called for me. We went to the nakamal, the Chief still singing the Tokka songs. He looked really happy. When we arrived at the nakamal, Jack had salvaged many small kava roots normally discarded in preparation and had enough for a few men to drink. The Chief was delighted. He stood to enact the Tokka dance around the sacred fire, thrusting a make-believe Tokka stick into the air as he sang the songs. We laughed at the simple, child-like innocence of this wise man.

He sat and talked animatedly about Tokka. I was able to ask him my questions. The Chief said that three people had been killed recently in the Tokka Festival. There are some dances where flat clubs are used, in the shape of birds with outstretched wings, in fighting routines. In one fighting sequence, he saw one boy killed when he was caught on the side of the head with the club and fell face down into the dust. Others have had their legs broken in other fighting enactment dances.

The Chief went on to say that it was a man from a special kastom lineage who killed the pigs at the end of the Tokka Festival. The pigs are laid end to end and he walks down the line giving two sharp blows to the head of each pig. The Tokka can only be danced by the men. The napen-napen can only be danced by the women. These are the two principal dances at the festival.

I asked the Chief for more information about the pads that the women beat during the napen-napen dance. He replied that the pads are called tennirup and they are filled with a sacred leaf known as nambregan. The Chief pointed to the edge of the nakamal, telling me that some of these plants grew there, but it was too dark to make out which plant he was actually pointing at.

The Chief said he would call a meeting with all of the chiefs who could host a Tokka Festival to come to Itabu to discuss who would host it in 2016. If Itabu was chosen, then men would have to travel long distances from many villages to clear large areas of the rain forest around the nakamal to make way for the dancers and spectators and to build a temporary Tokka village. The construction of this village begins well over a month prior to the festival starting. I secretly hoped that Itabu would not be chosen as it would mean a large area of beautiful forest would be put to the axe.

'We will kill a pig and drink kava; then all of the chiefs will talk to the spirit of the earth to see where the next festival will be held.'

The Chief repeated what he told me before about the modern Tokka not following the true kastom way. This obviously greatly upset him.

'This is because of the influence of the church and the West. Everybody who dances should be strictly kastom. Women should be bare breasted, with plain grass skirts and no face paint. The men should be naked except for nambas. Now they all wear Western clothing with their kastom dress. The shining ropes (tinsel), plastic flowers, headbands, boots and face painting are not kastom. This is not good, not true to Kassoso, our God who gave the Tokka dance to the people here at Itabu in this very nakamal generations ago.'

The Chief told the other men who were gathered in the nakamal about me standing in shit at the Tokka Festival and how well Iarueri danced to clean his boots. They all fell about laughing!

Jack called the Chief and I forward to drink kava. It was surprisingly strong. We sat in silence around the fire, praying to Kassoso. The Chief gave me the nod to leave, instructing me to leave my door open for Kassoso. Donald escorted me back to the village in the darkness so I wouldn't do anything stupid, like falling into a steaming volcanic vent a few yards from the path.

By 6.30 pm I was drenched in sweat and my clothes were wet through again. The night was airless, humid, hot and still. Mosquitoes found their way through the small holes in the torn mosquito net and bit me several times. I slept well, as I was awake all of the previous night at the Tokka Festival. There was no obvious sign of the Kassoso.

12th October 2012:
Meals on Wheels   Four Powerful Men
Kassoso Breath   Immaculate Conception

Nahu had placed fresh vermillion hibiscus flowers on the breakfast table for my hot tea and dog biscuits. Donald came instead of the Chief, explaining that his father had left early to go to the market. As Donald was privy to the tribal secrets and stories as High Chief in training, I asked him many questions, which he answered clearly and with ease.

He said, 'Iarueri, you have come a long way many times. You know how to respect the sacred nakamal; others do not. This is why we are telling you these things, as you are a Chief.'

A black and white dog ran through the restaurant; Donald hissed at it. It had a short stump of a tail. Donald said they often cut the tails off the dogs for hunting pigs, but leave the tails long on the lady dogs. Donald went on to say that when tinned fish was first introduced to the islands of Vanuatu the cannibals, realising the tins contained food, had no knives to break into them so they ripped them open with their teeth. They did the same with coconuts.

'We have very strong teeth,' Donald said laughingly.

When the first trucks arrived in Vanuatu the cannibals would stand in the road to smell for the fumes. Then, when they heard a truck coming, they would hide in the bushes following the truck until it stopped. They would creep up on the driver and club him to death, then eat him. I wondered if this would be the origin of meals on wheels! Donald said that Kassoso gave kava, pigs and chickens to the kastom people for ceremony.

'The kastom name for these sacred gifts is hissnowda. Kassos said that only the Chiefs can wear the black brow mark. In the past, people used different coloured volcanic clays to paint their faces and bodies but, after taking kava and killing a pig, the Kassoso told us to stop this practice. The kastom stories have been passed from father to son in the High Chief's lineage so are secret.'

Donald said that his father had told him these stories. 'My brothers or any of the other men do not know this information. In the past the water for the kastom kava ceremony was collected in a dried gourd, coconut or bamboo tubes. Today the men collect large plastic floats, washed up on the beach from the Taiwanese fishing boats, drilling a hole in the top so that they can fill with water; or we use plastic buckets. Kassoso do not like this.'

Donald answered many more of my questions about the Tokka. The big Chief from the Tokka is called Kio Apomis, meaning long man or big man. The long curved black rooster tail feathers he wears are called kio. The black feathers are worn by the Chief, the white feathers by his wife, Big Woman.

Donald said, 'As a Chief, you wear the black tail feather at the back of your head; Natu wears hers in the same place. Others of high rank wear them on the side of their heads. Any kastom person can wear a short white chicken feather but only behind their ear. Kassoso has said that only a High Chief is allowed to wear the black rooster tail feather or the eagle feather. No other person is permitted to do so.'

Donald then went on to explain about tribal hierarchy. 'The four most powerful men are the High Chief, Yeramanu, Yeni and Esheni. The High Chief rules like a king; the Yeramanu (Shaman) is like a priest or magician; the Yeni is like a small chief who looks after the people's needs, crops, kava, etc; and the Esheni is the head of the "kastom police" or security. He arrests and detains troublemakers. Sometimes one man will be the Yeramanu and Yeni. The High Chief is also known as Kio Apomis and he can make someone a Yeni, as the High Chief lineage is hereditary, passed from father to the firstborn son. Iarueri, your situation is different. Kassoso told the Chief that they wanted you to be made into a High Chief. They have started a new lineage through you for the West. It has never happened before. Kassoso are God; we do what they say. (As I have no children, this lineage passes to my nephew Aaron automatically at my death.)

'If my father becomes sick or too old and needs a stick to help him walk, then I will become High Chief. If my father dies, I become High Chief. If I was High Chief, I would make small Jack my Yeni. The Chief has two brothers (Note: in tribal culture, it is sometimes unclear if a "brother" is a blood relative or a man of equal grade or rank), Koata and Nikeow. Nikeow died. His son is also called Nikeow; he is the Esheni for this area. Sam's brother is Tom who lives in Vila. Tom is the firstborn to Koata but the Chief saw that Sam had a better connection with Spirit so he chose him as his Yeni.

'In the past village life at Itabu was quiet. Wild pigs and chickens passed through, especially at night. Now it is too noisy. The Kassoso do not like tourists, boots, Western clothing, radio music, etc. To see the Kassoso you must not swear, steal, fight or do anything immoral or unethical. This village is called Itabu because these things are taboo in the holy nakamal as it is the place of origin of our kastom way from Kassoso. It was also a sanctuary in times of warfare. Kassoso are special men.'

I asked Donald about the grass skirts the women wore at Tokka. 'The white grass skirts are called roas. The material is from a plant called bro or neue, a tree with yellow flowers. The bark is peeled and soaked in the sea or river then eased into "grass strips".'

I returned to my hut to get my towel and soap for a cold shower. As I pulled my towel off the bamboo partition inside my hut, a large black spider, about three inches across, fell to the floor at my feet. I said good morning to it, enquiring if it were vegetarian. I hoped it was; I didn't fancy it sinking its tooth into my neck as I slept. I washed some clothes, as the day was sunny and breezy, and hung some of my wet bedding out to dry. My wristwatch was full of condensation and had refused to work so I also left this out in the sun.

I was glad to have a stroll around the village in the sunshine. Those areas of earth that had not already dried out were now steaming in the heat. Today I felt really strong, powerful and alert. I was aware that a spiritual shift had taken place within me. I felt at one with nature and all life.

I walked down to the lower nakamal. Jack had begun to build a tree house in the big banyan tree on my last visit. It was now complete, with wooden steps leading up to it and curtains on the windows. When Natu and I visited Infitanna village to see a small Tokka dance in 2010, there were several small, but very old, tree houses in the great banyan trees. This was a village that tourists didn't visit as it was too remote. Tree houses are part of the ancient kastom culture in Tanna. In 2003 when I first visited Itabu village and surrounding areas, there were no tree houses in this part of the island. Now, everywhere you look, they are in most of the big trees to try to encourage tourists. (The Health and Safety brigade would try to stop this practice. Risk is character building.)

Likewise, when I first visited this area, Itabu was completely different to what it is now. All of the original buildings have been demolished, mostly due to cyclonic activity and because they are made from natural materials from the rain forest which only tend to have a limited lifespan of about two years before they start to rot in the humidity. Itabu is slowly but steadily growing in size. The old paraffin

Tree house at Itabu.

hurricane lamps have been replaced with plastic solar powered lamps. When the new highway reaches Itabu, life in this tranquil village will be thrust into Western materialism, bringing tourist buses, probably leaving a trail of litter everywhere. I pray to Kassoso to protect this sacred place, the birthplace of the Dragon Men.

There are also anomalies at Itabu. Most of the water pipes that were installed in 2005 have been buried beneath the ground, yet some of these pipes that cross the stony main track lie on the surface for trucks to run over. If any pipes are to be buried, it should be these! Some of the pipes crossing the road are suspended between long bamboo poles.

I returned to my hut, since the ground was getting too hot to walk on in my bare feet. Of course, the locals are in bare feet most of the time, but they are used to it from walking barefoot as toddlers. Being barefoot enables us to connect correctly with the Earth Mother, whereas modern shoes, which are synthetic, disconnect us from Her.

Donald called for me at 11.30 to have some fresh cucumber and tomato. I guessed that the Chief had returned from the market. I was unsure if this was a pleasant snack or lunch. It turned out to be lunch. The Chief arrived about 2.30 pm and called me for more questions and answers. As usual, I had a lot of questions I needed to run past him.

We spoke of tribal divine names. The Chief said that Majikjiki, Yeramanu, Tangarua, Kumesen, Yasur and Kassoso are all different names for God. The names can be changed with the exception of Kassoso. This name cannot be changed; it must remain true.

'Iarueri, Kassoso gave the first breath to Tangarua. His first breath was given to Majikjiki. His first breath was given to you. Your breath is for Kassoso. A father and mother give their first breath to their son. Kassoso is my father. No other country in the world knows this secret story of Kassoso, except on Tanna Island and Manannan's Island. Why is this, Iarueri?'

I didn't know what to say at this profound statement. The Chief smiled at me, his heart full of love, and said, 'Because I gave you the true story, my brother.'

I felt somewhat emotional with this comment, blinking back tears and swallowing hard. The Chief said that we had upset Kassoso by beginning the first ceremony, then breaking off to go to the Tokka Festival.

'We have to start again to say "sorry" and to make a new road to reconnect. We need to kill a pig and take kava tonight in the nakamal to do this. In their true form Kassoso are spirit men; they are not physical. They come out of the volcano and live in the jungle. You cannot see them with ordinary eyes so we need to make a road to them slowly, so they know our intentions, so they can give us their power. We will kill a pig or black chicken for Kassoso to eat. The spirit of the pig is in its blood. When the pig's blood soaks into the ground, the pig's spirit makes a road to the volcano for Kassoso to travel along more easily. When Kassoso feed on pig or chicken, they take on the form of a physical man, so can touch you. They can also kill you. After they have eaten they are less strong so it is safer to touch them. Iarueri, I have money but Kassoso need to know that you provided the pig for tonight. Will you pay for it?'

I gave the Chief the amount he needed. The Chief smiled and left immediately.

A crimson and black Majikjiki bird flitted from the vermillion hibiscus flowers, drinking their nectar, as I made my way back to my leaf hut. It had grown overcast and humid again. I spent the remainder of my time in prayer to Kassoso to await the call to the nakamal.

I connected to Spirit in meditation and asked what the connection was between dragons and Kassoso. Without warning, I suddenly found myself at the nakamal, sitting with the Chief, Nikwei and Donald around the fire at dusk. The Chief indicated for me to remain silent. A few men who had finished drinking kava then left. The four of us were alone. The Chief shared his shell of kava with me so we could call Kassoso. Then, at the edge of the nakamal, I saw the Kassoso coming in their hundreds. It was astonishing! They seemed agitated for some reason. My companions seemed afraid.

The leader of Kassoso indicated for me to follow him where, at a certain point in the nakamal, he thrust his staff into the ground, causing it to open up into a volcanic vent. As the ground gave way I fell downwards into the molten magma, followed by Kassoso. After a moment of reorienting myself, I saw a golden dragon chained within the depths of the volcano. This surprised me, as I had not expected to experience something of this nature in a strong indigenous kastom culture. This dragon was straining against chains which caused them to remain taut and strong, as he was giving these restraints his vitality. I asked for permission to enter into his sacred space, gently persuading him to reverse backwards into the dungeon-like enclosure, so pressure was released from the chains. Then I felt the Dragon Sword in my hand so smashed the chains to release him. The golden dragon rose upwards through the volcano, cascading magma then lava off him as he broke through the surface into the crater. Kassoso flowed after him like a swarm of honeybees after their Queen.

The dragon breathed the fresh air once more and opened his wings to the night air, raising his head to cry a cry that would wake the dead and reach far out into the universe. The volcano erupted, incinerating all in its path that was not sacred, including the black magic that was used to constrain this magnificent creature in the first place. It was free. Kassoso wept and danced. The dragon became transformed into a dragon of living fire. It called to me to ride upon him as his rider. I too became a being of living fire as we descended back into the molten seas connecting to the great Guardians of the Sacred Iron Crystals at the centre of our world, then passing on to a place where the magma was trapped and compressed.

Eventually the compression released, enabling us to break free, emerging at Dragon's Gate (Cronk Sumark) on the Isle of Man (the place where Maggie and I were betrothed). Kassoso poured out into the Manx landscape. The Dragon of Fire roared to reactivate and awaken the ancient guardians of this portal. Dragons came through the Star Gate once again, reconnecting Mann to the star nations.

We returned back to Yasur the way we came. I dismounted to see a large figure of fire standing at the rim of the volcano. It was Tangarua. He bowed gracefully to me and called me his son. I felt very emotional. He then took his rightful place upon the dragon and flew off through a Star Gate into the great void of the universe. I knew without any doubt that he was one of the great Dragon Lords.

I came out of meditation and waited outside of my hut for the Chief to call. I saw an eagle circling over the nakamal. This definitely was a good sign! All of the plants were covered in a fine coating of black volcanic ash, which is not good in the lungs. Many people have breathing and lung problems around the volcano.

When the Chief came, I took my grade belt with me as I wanted to make the right connection to the nakamal, pig, kava and sacred fire to bring these energies to the belt. On our way to the nakamal, the Chief almost stood on a discarded open tuna tin on the trail, which was partially burnt in a fire, but with the ring pull lid sticking up like a sharp knife. I called the Chief over and said that if anyone stood on this with their bare feet it would cut them deeply. He thanked me for showing him the tin and picked it up. As we passed through Donald's village, he called Donald's son, little Wai Wai, giving him the tin, telling him clearly to put the tin somewhere safe so nobody would step on to it. The Chief and I continued on to the nakamal. I turned to see Wai Wai throw the tin into the bushes!

We arrived at the nakamal, followed by a dog with a tail and a dew claw on her back leg ripped out and hanging loosely on a small piece of skin. A stranger arrived to speak to the Chief. The Chief introduced me to the man who was called Steven. He was about mid-50s in age with a big white and black beard. His moustache completely covered his mouth. I wondered how he ate and drank. He was a strong kastom man so, by the size of his beard, he must have been a chief who held a high grade. Steven spoke good English and told me different things about the kastom way and said that the nakamal has four paths leading into and out of it.

'The church stole this idea for their cross,' he said crossly.

Steven asked me where Natu was, so I explained that it was too expensive for both of us to travel at this time. He and the Chief then went into a personal discussion about some problem that he had. If men have a problem, they always come to the Chief at the nakamal to discuss their situation, or the Chief drinks kava with them in their village nakamal.

Donald arrived with the pig, a very small pig, more like a piglet. Another man arrived with the kava. The pig squealed the entire time. It and the kava were laid side by side in the centre of the nakamal. I laid my grade belt across both to make that energetic connection. Then the dog had a go at nipping the pig so Donald kicked the dog away. The man who brought the kava killed the pig, its blood and spirit seeping back into the dark earth, back to Kassoso.

Another stranger arrived to report to the Chief, telling him about the ritual slaughter of the pigs after the Tokka. He was very excited and animated in his story. All of the men present were spellbound by the tale. He said he saw 220 pigs killed, one after the other, all in a straight line. More were killed later, he said.

Donald sent two small boys off into the forest to cut sticks with machetes to cook the meat over the fire, whilst another boy got the fire going. Others prepared kava. Another boy turned up pushing his stick car, making a lot of noise. Both the Chief and Donald told him to go, as it was kava time and a time of silence. One boy climbed a coconut tree, placing his feet in the notches cut previously, pulling down the coconuts. He must have climbed about 50 feet.

Steven turned to me and said, 'See, here we climb trees in our bare feet. In the West you need boots with nails. Everything here is free. All of our crops are free. We just keep harvesting and planting. If you are prepared to work and sweat, you don't need money. This is what the Christians call paradise.'

Steven went to sit with the other men to talk. The Chief had indicated that he wanted to talk to me privately. We sat by the sacred fire – the place of God. Flying foxes wheeled through the night sky calling to each other, cicadas began their evening choir practice and fireflies chased each other through the tree canopies. I could smell fragrant perfume from tropical flowers. Moths searched for them to drink their nectar. Yasur volcano boomed, lighting the night sky with hues of red, followed by copious amounts of thick white smoke which swirled around the nakamal when the wind was in the right direction.

I pushed my bare feet into the dark sacred earth at the side of the fire, enjoying the aromatic blue wood smoke as it curled around my body. Children laughed in the distance; a baby cried; a dog barked across the valley. I felt totally at peace in this holy place. I was aware of Donald sharpening his machete on a stone to butcher the pig. A deep silence fell upon the nakamal even though I could hear the soft voices of the men talking.

The Chief touched my hand to break my trance-like state. He smiled at me, half closing his eyes as he was engulfed in wood smoke.

'Iarueri, I want to tell you our creation story in full. I have given you bits and pieces, little by little, but now you must understand the true story. It will help you to make a road to travel along to meet Kassoso. This is a secret story; it must not be told to anyone else.'

The Creation Myth

The Chief looked into my eyes, shifting on his log like a true storyteller, ready to begin. He cleared his throat, 'In the beginning, a God man and God woman came from the stars. The God man was the first great High Chief called Tangarua, who was the first Kassoso. He created Tanna Island from the volcano, as he was of the sea in his first form as the black and white sea snake. He then came on land and built the first dwelling which became this village, Itabu. It was taboo, or forbidden, to all that was not sacred.

'The God woman was called Pieria. One day Tangarua went into the jungle to cut down an area to make a garden, cutting his left hand badly. The only water nearby was what was contained in a hollow in the nawaias tree. Here he washed his bleeding hand, filling the waterhole with his sacred blood. Some time later, Pieria came along and, being thirsty, drank the water from the nawaias tree not knowing it contained divine blood. She soon became pregnant, giving birth to twin sons (immaculate conception!). The firstborn was white and called Majikjiki; he was the white serpent. The second born was black and called Kumesen; he was the black serpent.

'Pieria went on to have another ten sons, twelve in total. All of the God woman's sons were different, some were white, black, brown, red and yellow. All took wives

The sacred
Nawaias tree.

when of age. Majikjiki had a wife called Sapai and they had many children (the Chief did not say where the women came from!).

'Iarueri, you know Majikjiki by the name of Manannan and you are from his lineage being a reincarnation of his firstborn son. Majikjiki and Kumesen are known around the world by different names as they are our first ancestors. When Tangarua Kassoso realised that he was now mortal and would die, he instructed Pieria to bury him when he did, but his skull had to be above ground, face up and be covered in volcanic clay (was this the origin of skull veneration in the South Pacific?). When Tangarua died, Pieria did as instructed, covering the God man's skull in clay. From his right eye sprang holy waters, which were contained within woven wild canes. From his left eye sprang the first coconut tree and the rest of creation.

'As Majikjiki was the firstborn son, he inherited the God lineage after Tangarua's death and became guardian of the sacred pool, a holy place maintaining the link back to the stars. It was forbidden for anyone else to go there.

'Itabu was known by some as the Garden of Eden. One day, whilst Pieria was working in her garden, she heard the laughter of the boys as they splashed noisily in the holy waters. She ran from her garden with her axe. By chance, Kumesen saw his mother coming so he and his brothers fled into the mountains, leaving Majikjiki to face the wrath of his mother alone. Pieria saw that the sacred waters were dirty and contaminated so their connection back to the stars was broken and lost. The lineage had lost its immortality. She was furious. Pieria asked Majikjiki: had his brothers been in the pool? He denied it, but Pieria knew he was lying and shouted that, not only had be broken kastom law, but he had broken spiritual law also. She took up her axe, cutting down the wild canes, causing the holy waters to flow into the earth. Majikjiki tried desperately to stop the flow of water by pushing over two trees in the form of an "X" but it had no effect. The sacred waters were lost.

'At this point, the oceans started to bubble up from the earth and the skies grew dark with storm clouds. It rained heavily for many days and nights, causing widespread flooding. Majikjiki and his family built a great wooden boat that the early Christians called the Ark, calling to every creature, two by two, so they wouldn't be drowned. The non-kastom people laughed at Majikjiki, ridiculing him and his family. As the waters rose and became deeper, destroying villages and gardens, the people cried out to Majikjiki to save them, asking for a place on his boat. Majikjiki refused as they had no respect for Spirit. Only the 12 tribes and their families were permitted.

'Kumesen, the black serpent, and his family stayed on Tanna Island at a high place where they were safe. From this vantage point, they saw three massive tidal waves form which swept across the face of the earth in three different directions, lifting and carrying Majikjiki and his boat to the West. The Ark was swept to Aneityum, Futuna, Erromango and the rest of the islands of Vanuatu. At regular intervals a pigeon, known as a quira, was set free to locate land (because of this sacred service, no one is permitted to hunt or kill a quira except a High Chief).

'At the sighting of each land mass a brother and his family were dropped off to start a new race – the yellows in the Orient; the browns in Asia; the blacks in Africa; the reds in America; the olive-skinned to Palestine, Egypt and Greece (this is why Prince Philip is venerated with God-like status as he belongs to the Greek Royal bloodline going back to the first ancestors, whereas others have lost the true lineage over time); finally coming to rest on a powerful small island off the coast of England. This became Majikjiki's home and the place of his descendants, the descendants of the White Serpent. Over time he became known as Manannan and his island is known now as Manannan's Island (Isle of Man). Because Majikjiki was adrift upon the seas for a long time, God provided fish for them to eat. The fish became one of his sacred symbols which was stolen by the Christians. Over time the Ark rotted and returned back into the earth.

'After the floods disappeared Kumesen and his tribe waited for many generations for the return of the White Serpent to reunite the lineage of the two twins. Over time they kept the secret story alive, passing it down from one High Chief to the next. The story focussed upon the three tidal waves, as this was what Kumesen had experienced from his vantage point, so this image became the secret symbol that would indicate the true White Serpent when he returned.' (This symbol is the triskele, the national sigil of the Isle of Man. It is also found in Greece, Sicily and Scandinavia.)

"Restaurant" at Itabu from my leaf hut.

I said to the Chief that this story is so amazing that you couldn't have made it up!
He laughed.

'Brother,' I said, hanging my head, staring at the smouldering embers of the
nakamal fire, 'I am troubled. There are two Isles of Man. The other is on the
west coast of Ireland called Inishmaan, one of the Aran Islands in Galway Bay.
They also honour Manannan as God. In fact, when I was in the Aran Islands
some years ago, Manannan revealed himself to me very powerfully. How do you
know that the true White Serpent is not a man from this island rather than the
Isle of Man?'

The Chief smiled, giving me the "father to son" look, 'Iarueri, you are sitting here
now; he is not. You are chosen.'

I felt stupid, but needed to ask that question. I felt much better for this clarity. Over
the last nine years, the Chief and Donald have given me this secret information, bit
by bit, privy only to the High Chief lineage. At times I found it contradictory and
confusing, until today when it all fitted together like a jigsaw puzzle. I asked the
Chief's permission to reveal this amazing story to the West but he refused, saying it
was "secret".

The Chief and I were called to drink kava. We called upon Tamaffa and to
Kassoso that we may make a path to meet them. The kava was very strong. By
this time the pig had been butchered and its flesh and organs skewered on sticks
over the fire. The flesh was put into the flames to singe and burn off the skin and
hair and to pull off the hooves. A boy arrived from Donald's camp, carrying a
dirty yellow plastic washing up bowl containing rice, cabbage and chicken with
one spoon that the men would share. I was offered first pickings. The Chief
pulled out a chicken leg for me. It was tasty but bloody at the bone. I threw it
secretly to the dog.

Then I was called to leave. Even though I had paid for the pig and it was for our
ceremony, I never got to eat any of it. As I left, I drew my grade belt through the
smoke of the fire and the cooking pig meat to make that energetic connection.
Donald and I returned to the restaurant where I had two more chicken legs and rice
for dinner. I wondered if the Chief had bought a small pig and the chicken with my
money? The Chief had said that, to connect to Kassoso, you can either use a pig or
chicken. Even though I ate chicken, it wasn't killed in ritual at the nakamal for its
blood and spirit to make a road to Kassoso.

Land of Crystal and Fire   Leaf Shelter
Kassoso came in the Night

Up at 5.30 am. As it is the beginning of the wet season, everything is damp and humid, although the wet season doesn't officially begin until November through to February. My bar of soap could not dry out so it had turned to jelly and green mould was growing on my bed sheets.

After my tea, dog biscuits and nature identical jam for breakfast, the Chief arrived for our morning question and answer session, which I always looked forward to. The Chief was smiling broadly, saying that he had had a powerful dream where Kassoso came and told him they were happy that we did the ceremony last night. They are prepared to connect now. He asked if I had had a dream, but I hadn't. The Chief said Kassoso told him to make a camp in a different place this time on the edge of the nakamal opposite the banyan tree. I felt concerned about this, as the other men would know what we were doing. The Chief said he would tell the men to keep away. He said that Kassoso had promised to come tonight at midnight to give their secrets. He continued to say that his father had also come to him in his dream and said that Kassoso had not been ready to touch a strange white man before.

'Iarueri, they now recognise that you are the son of Majikjiki and the grandson of Tangarua so will offer to you the neape, their sacred stick. After that connection, they want another ceremony of gratitude to be done. That will be the end. After that, Kassoso will come to you in your dreams and visions to bring you insights and instructions. At 3 pm we will make a small shelter. You are to sleep at the front by the door and I at the back this time. Kassoso will present their neape for you to touch to give you their power. Midnight is the main time for Kassoso to come. Kassoso want you to know this, Iarueri,' the Chief said, smiling.

'I will tell the others not to come to the nakamal tonight, except for Donald and Jack. They alone will prepare the kava for us. When you touch the neape, it is the end, the last ceremony.'

The Chief was very focussed and clear this time. The last time we attempted to connect with Kassoso he was clearly afraid and kept procrastinating.

'Iarueri, Kassoso said no fighting or quarrelling is permitted now with Natu or anyone else. You have to live a life of peace. When a pig or chicken is killed, the spirit of the animal goes ahead to Kassoso to tell Kassoso that we wait to talk to them. Kassoso are peaceful men; they do not like aggression, violence or bad energy. That keeps them away. They can kill if circumstances are difficult but usually they disappear into the night, never to return. Brother, you must have a good heart, peace and compassion to draw to you the path to Kassoso. Once this connection has been made, Kassoso can come to Manannan's Island. I don't know this for sure, as I have only ever known them to be at Itabu. I don't know what Kassoso will say to you. We have to make the connection slowly so they can get used to the idea and come to meet us. Once Kassoso has made the connection with you, they will tell you their secrets and stay with you. I am very happy with this.'

'Iarueri, when the Kassoso arm came through your window, even though you were afraid, you had the choice of running away or holding their hand. This was another test for you. As you had the courage to take hold of the hand, Kassoso knew you were ready for the next initiation. Had you chosen to run away or not take hold of their hand, you would not have made any further connection with Kassoso ever again. When you are in Manannan's Island, if I die, or Donald dies, or any of my family die, Kassoso will tell you. If you die, Kassoso will come to me and tell me. They will tell you what to do in your life to help you. My father in spirit said he is very happy also.'

After a pause to drink some water, the Chief continued, 'Iarueri, I will not touch the neape tonight. This rite is for you alone at this time. I will connect with Kassoso to do this at a later date. These are the instructions from my father. We are both old men now, Iarueri (I disagreed with this statement!). We have stopped fighting and need to be responsible with high ethics and morals. Donald is still a boy; he enjoys playing games. Donald will have his turn at my death. Kassoso brought Natu and you together to marry. Kassoso will guide you both in your lives. Go to your hut now, Iarueri, to pray to Kassoso and prepare for later. Try to sleep and make contact with Kassoso so they will talk to you tonight. Brother, we have been preparing for this moment for many years. It has been slow progress, but necessary, as a test of your endurance, commitment and dedication to all of the challenges and difficulties you have faced. It is time! I will tell no one about these plans; it is our secret. Kassoso want you to eat a clam for lunch today. I will send Donald's boy to the market at the sea to get one for you. It is really good eating.'

I was somewhat horrified at the prospect of eating shellfish, especially as it will have to be carried for a couple of hours in the heat. How fresh would it be anyway on the stall in the hot sun, I wondered. I voiced my concerns about becoming sick, especially for tonight, as I needed to be strong and alert. The Chief assured me I would not be sick so I had to trust Spirit now.

After a shower, I returned to my hut to prepare for the magical encounter with Kassoso. I was amazed at the sophisticated words and phrases that the Chief and Donald used on this visit.

It rained as I began my meditation.

I journeyed shamanically to the forbidden pool of Itabu and called Nuie, its guardian, for permission to enter sacred space. The day became night with the reflection of the full moon falling across the surface of the pool. This reflection created a portal which opened to reveal a tunnel of spiralling fire, leading downwards into the Lower World.

At first I was wary so called in my spirit allies, who entered the tunnel of fire ahead of me, so I knew it was safe to proceed. We journeyed downwards through the ribbed tunnel of intense fire until we came to a large cavern system deep underground. This landscape was created out of dark crystal and fire. Magma cascaded in torrents, which plunged as if it were "waterfalls" flowing into a huge magma river, which flowed on to an ocean of magma. My belly became physically hot at this point. It seemed as though there was no beginning or end to this phenomenon. As far as I could see in every direction, I saw cliffs of dark crystal, magma and fire. It was a place of indescribable raw power.

As I reoriented and grounded myself into these new surroundings, I noticed a narrow winding path that led upwards into a crystal rock face of a distant mountain, where there was an opening that looked like a mine shaft from where I stood. On either side of this opening were two massive clear crystal pillars. We walked to this entrance where we were stopped by several veiled figures, wearing robes of fire. They enquired of our business. After explaining who we were and why we were in their realm, they allowed us to pass. We entered into another series of caverns which were temple-like.

My allies instructed me to enter into a chamber on my left, which I found to be a place of cleansing and transformation. I had to pass through a short wide tunnel of fire. As I entered I felt my body being incinerated at all levels, consumed by sacred fire. I emerged cleansed and purified. I felt clean, light and buoyant. I began to grow and expand into a crystal being, fire danced through my veins instead of blood. I felt powerful and invincible. I was aware that my Kassoso tattoo had lit up and was shining like a badge of office in my energy body.

I was guided by my allies into another temple space which was stunning in its raw beauty and power. Huge walls of dark crystal were lit from within by flowing rivers of red magma. Dragons of black crystal and red fire hung from the crevices of the rock faces. Magma cascaded from holes in distant black crystal mountains; yet, surprisingly, this place was not uncomfortably hot or held any toxic fumes. Within its central plateau was a temple-like structure formed in living golden flames, similar to the Greek Parthenon. High above this was a light, so intense and bright that it shone like a subterranean sun, and from this a beam of golden light reached into the golden temple space. This was clearly a throne room. As my eyes adjusted to the intensity of the light, I saw a crystal throne with a figure sitting upon it. I was told he was the King of Kassoso. I felt his power and authority but had difficulty in seeing him. I knelt in respect before the King. A stick, his stick, touched me on my shoulder and I heard the words, 'You kneel before no man. We may be different, but we are equal. Stand.'

I stood. The King spoke again, 'What do you want from us?'

I replied, 'To receive the ancient wisdom of your race that will help me in my healing work. I also ask for a blessing for my wife, Natu Elin.'

There was a moment of silence. I then became aware of others standing behind the throne.

'You seek no power or treasures?'

'No, my brother. The only treasures I seek are the gifts of Spirit.'

I was dismissed instantly, returning with my allies to the forbidden pool to integrate within my physical body. I was unsure if I had said the right thing or not; I simply spoke the truth from my heart.

The timing was perfect, as the Chief arrived at my hut minutes after I had written up this shamanic journey in my journal. I told him of my vision. He was delighted and said that everything was ready for tonight. He asked me for more money to buy a big pig for the ceremony of gratitude after we had made contact with Kassoso. I gave him the money needed, which was a substantial amount and hoped I would have enough Vatu left for the rest of my stay. I trusted the Chief, my brother, completely and knew he would never cheat me. The Chief went off to buy his pig.

The sun came out so I hung wet bedding and clothes out to dry. They soon began to steam. I was called early again for lunch at 11.15. When I arrived at the restaurant, I saw a huge meal cooked for me. The clam was on the plate along with rice, noodles, tomatoes and carrots. The clam was white meat, rubbery and full of grit or sand.

There was no taste. I remembered eating this meat on a previous visit, wondering what it was. I spent the rest of the day in my hut, contemplating and praying to Kassoso. At 2 pm I ventured out to have a piddle and I saw a flying fox circling high in the sky above my hut. This was a seriously good omen, I thought, as they are rarely out in daylight.

I made a couple more shamanic journeys back into the great realm below of crystal and fire. Each time I went the landscape revealed more of its secrets and details to me. I thought it was a pity that the path was so circuitous from my arrival point to the concealed temple. As soon as I thought this, the pathway changed to where I had placed my focus and intention, creating viaducts of pure crystal that spanned the seething molten rivers below. I looked into the matrix of the cliff face, seeing fire pulsing through the crystal like volcanic blood. I imagined a hole opening up in the crystalline matrix so I could put my arm into it and it happened instantly, returning back to its normal form when I withdrew my focus and intent.

I realised that, in this realm, I had to be very careful about what I focussed upon and what I desired. It was a huge responsibility knowing that whatever I thought I materialised instantly. I felt really uncomfortable with this power so decided to return, since I didn't want to harm anything or anyone through an unfocussed casual thought.

I looked at my alarm clock, because my wristwatch was still wet with condensation and had decided to sulk. It was 3 pm. I waited until dark but there was no sign of the Chief. I stood in the darkness outside the restaurant waiting for him, or someone sent by him to take me to the nakamal. I knew the way, as I had been there countless times, but the Chief insisted I was escorted each time because he didn't want me falling into a volcanic vent.

I heard a couple of young boys laughing in the kitchen area of the restaurant. I walked up to the open window and peered inside. They had a torch lit so couldn't see me outside in the bushes. They had found the jar of Pakistan nature identical flavoured strawberry jam and were helping themselves to it, with their sticky fingers and a teaspoon. Then they found a container of sugar. They put several spoons of sugar in a plastic tumbler and poured water into it, stirring it with a spoon, then drank it. They heard someone coming so turned the torch off, put the jam back on the shelf and ran off into the darkness.

As I waited, I connected shamanically with my dragon and called him to me. When he came he was different. Instead of his usual reptilian form, he was a magnificent beast of crystal and fire. I took my place astride him as a Dragon Rider and we flew to the nakamal. I called to Kassoso. We flew to the realm of crystal and fire and, as before, my belly became physically very hot. We returned to Itabu.

The Chief arrived at 5 pm. He apologised for the delay, explaining that the shelter had been built. He had to go off to see a man about something but would be back shortly. We eventually arrived at the nakamal for 5.30 pm. There were several men there, including Nikwei. All of the men knew what the Chief and I were going to do, as they were discussing it in hushed tones, looking at me like the condemned man. I don't know if they considered me brave or a fool!

Donald and Nikwei had built the shelter for us at the perimeter of the nakamal, where Kassoso had indicated. The Chief called me to the banyan tree to show me the tumbled white quartz stones that I had sent him from the Isle of Man some years ago. Some of these stones were becoming encapsulated within the bark of the banyan tree itself. I wondered what the reaction would be from anthropologists or geologists in the far distant future if they found these stones, alien to this country. What made up theories and stories they would concoct to publish a scientific paper!

The evening air was full of a heavy perfume from the cascading flowers, hanging from the banyan trees, of a species of hoya. I commented on the wonderful perfume, so a man went to the flowers and cut one for me with his machete, presenting it to me at the fire. The flower head was a collection of smaller cream flowers that had red centres and a waxy coating. Some of the men wore these flowers in their hair. (Perfumed flowers are the highest expression of perfection in the plant kingdom as crystals are in the mineral kingdom.)

The Chief and Nikwei drank kava together, praying to Tamaffa, Majikjiki and Kassoso that I may connect with Kassoso tonight. The Chief said I was not to drink kava tonight. I was told to return to the restaurant for my meal, which was a whole cucumber and dog biscuits with tea. Nahu ran off into the darkness, returning in 10 minutes, panting, with a new jar of Pakistan nature identical flavoured strawberry jam. The boys had obviously cleaned out the jar earlier!

After my meal, I stood outside the restaurant in the darkness admiring the clear night sky with its myriad of stars. Thankfully, there were no clouds or rain. The Chief had told me not to wear a watch, any perfume or anything Western that may startle Kassoso. I kept my glasses, as I needed them, realising that this wasn't ideal. As I waited I shamanically tuned into the dragon consciousness of the planet. I saw a huge black crystal-like dragon emerging from Yasur volcano and was aware of hundreds of other dragons emerging around the globe. It is time for the dragons to take back control of the skies once more.

Laughter rang out in one of the huts at the edge of the village. A communal fire burned between the huts for the women to cook for several families. The wood smoke seemed to search me out and curl around my body. The distant mountain range was no longer covered in low cloud or mist for the first time in days. They stood out sharp and clear, black against the night sky. I watched several shooting stars. A couple of fireflies danced around my head, then flew off to some nearby bushes. I saw the shadowy forms of flying foxes passing before the shining stars, then noticed a satellite – a pinprick of bright light moving steadily across the heavens. Except for the early mosquitoes, it was a perfect South Pacific evening.

Boys saw me waiting in the bushes so ran off to tell Nahu. She gave them a solar lamp to put in the restaurant for me. I was quite happy standing in the darkness, but this was done as an act of kindness, so I thanked the boys. After they had left, I moved back into the shadows of the bushes, noticing the return of the two jam thieves who couldn't see me. They found the new jar of nature identical jam, dipping their sticky fingers into it several times and licking the jam off. One boy sneezed heavily into the jar. (Memo to self: scoop off nasal mucus before applying jam to dog biscuits tomorrow.) The boys made several trips in and out whilst I waited.

After a considerable wait, the Chief arrived at 8 pm. He said we had to wait for the village to go to sleep before we go to meet the secret men. He said he would call for me at the right time, so I should return to my hut and pray to Kassoso. Several dogs barked. The Chief said this was a good sign. Yasur volcano was quiet tonight, not exploding as before. Yet the night sky still glowed a deep red from his sacred lava and flames.

The Chief called for me at 10 pm. We made our way silently through the sleeping village along the jungle trails in torchlight to the nakamal and to our shelter. The shelter was a simple construction, built on a slight slope, of branches cut into poles in the form of an A frame, then palm leaves woven and tied around the frame, so it was virtually camouflaged. The doorway was covered by a palm leaf which you pushed through to enter and exit. Inside was hung a blue plastic mosquito net from the main cross pole and upon the earth a couple of pandanus mats. Two small pillows and a large pink satin sheet were laid on top of the mats for us. We removed our footwear and I took off my glasses, settling down for the night. We lay side by side, covered by the pink satin sheet. I prayed that we would not be found dead in the morning in this compromising situation!

Initially, I was disappointed about the plastic mosquito net but, as the night drew on, I was very thankful for it as the mosquitoes were insistent in trying to feed off us, at least their constant whining was on the outside so we were rarely bitten. I stared at the clear night sky through the gaps in the leaf fronds, watching the flying foxes flying overhead, some landing noisily in the trees foraging for fruit. I was fascinated watching the fireflies which were like miniature balls of fire racing through the undergrowth and across the nakamal.

We settled down to sleep. The Chief's breath was heavy with the smell of tobacco and kava and, once asleep, he snored so loudly it could have woken the dead, interspersed with impressive explosions of flatulence. During a lull in his snoring and farting, I dozed off sleeping lightly, then was woken by a movement in the undergrowth next to the shelter. I assumed it was the Chief creeping out of the shelter for a piddle but he snored at the side of me. I was alert instantly! I stared up through the gaps in the leaf fronds at the night sky, the stars so bright they cast an eerie light that lit the jungle. Then I saw someone, or something, standing next to me on the outside of the shelter. It was Kassoso! I saw Kassoso bend over slightly, peering back at me through the palm fronds. He held a staff, possibly four to five feet in length, in his right hand, directing the top of the staff with his left hand, prodding the end through the palm fronds towards my face, rustling the leaves to alert me to his presence. He wanted me to know he was there. This was it, I thought: the final initiation after nine years of preparation!

I saw his outline clearly against the night sky – that of a Ni-Van with closely cropped hair. He appeared to be naked. I couldn't see anything else, as it was just too dark. Unfortunately, the plastic mosquito net prevented the neape from reaching me. I tried desperately to get my hand under the net to reach up for the stick, but I couldn't manage it. I took hold of the end of the stick which was pushing the mosquito net towards my face, feeling its rough hewn texture through the plastic. I took hold of the stick firmly. As soon as I had touched the neape, Kassoso pulled it away and left, disappearing into the darkness.

On our last attempt to meet Kassoso in 2010, they made a peculiar sound as they approached our camp. Tonight, they were silent. The Chief slept on unaware of the encounter. I called silently from my heart to Kassoso, asking that they would return for a second attempt as, by this time, I had loosened the plastic netting so my arm was free. I left my arm and hand out as long as I could trying to ignore the persistent mosquito bites, but in the end withdrew it inside the net. I sensed that this encounter had taken place at midnight as the Chief said it would do.

14th October 2012:
Shared Clothes   Sick Baby   Spirit Stones   Maggots

I spent the rest of the night awake, praying to Kassoso to return but they did not come back. I felt bitterly disappointed. Part of me was still sceptical about Kassoso, so I prayed to Majikjiki to bring to me unequivocal proof of the authenticity of Kassoso and what my role is in a way I can understand. Yasur volcano coughed several times throughout the night. In the early hours both the Chief and I crept out of our shelter to urinate, returning to sleep. It was amazing how much you could see by starlight. There was no sign of the moon.

We slept fitfully until dawn. The Chief's cell phone suddenly rang! I was horrified that he would have even considered bringing it for such a rare spiritual encounter. He apologised, leaving the shelter to talk in his native tongue. The Chief left, no doubt on another mission of mercy. Soon after, Donald arrived to escort me back to the restaurant for breakfast. Nahu had left hot tea, jam and dog biscuits out on the table by 5.30 am and yes, I did forget to scoop off the nasal mucous left by the boys, so drank copious quantities of hot tea to wash down the slime.

The Chief arrived in due course for our question and answer session. The Chief said Kassoso came to him in his dreams; he saw them clearly. He also said that his father came to him, making a noise and reaching out his hand, but he couldn't touch him. His father was very happy, he said. The Chief laughed, his eyes sparkling. I told the Chief of my experience and my concerns about the plastic mosquito net. The Chief said that we would try again tonight but, if we didn't use the mosquito net, we would both be badly bitten.

The Chief became excited and animated, rolling his eyes. 'Iarueri, did you hear the flying fox directly above us last night in the tree? That was Kassoso. There is no fruit on that tree, so he came to peer down into our leaf shelter.'

He laughed again, slapping his thigh. The Chief added that he slept better in the shelter than he did in his own house. He said he felt relaxed and strong. 'Iarueri, tonight you drink small kava and eat pig. We have to "kill" the power of Kassoso so they will be less strong. When they eat pig and drink kava, they lose a lot of their power as they materialise into human form. They know us now. They will come again. When they come tonight, put your hand under the mosquito net and reach up to touch their stick. It is important to touch the stick with your hand so they can give you their power. They know that we have both made an effort to make a road to them. I am going off now to see a boy about a pig for tonight and to make the preparations for the ceremony. I am very happy, brother!'

The Chief left, laughing. I went for a shower but there was no water. What often happens is that, in the catchment area in the mountains, water washes down fine silt which clogs the pipes feeding the tanks. Donald sent two boys off into the mountains to clear the pipes. The term "boy" is often used for a young man who may or may not be married. Likewise, they use the term to "swim" when they mean to wash. Once you understood the words they used in the right context, there was very little conversation that needed an interpreter after several days. I heard a pig squealing in the direction of Donald's encampment, so I knew its fate for tonight.

I find it fascinating that the kastom people, male and female, share the same clothes, especially the tops. One day I saw the Chief wearing a particular top, then the following day Donald was wearing it, followed over the next few days by Jack, Nahu and others, before it was washed. If someone takes their shirt or coat off to play football or work in their garden, any passing person who needs that garment will take it and wear it. When they no longer need that item, they will leave it for someone else to wear. Most clothes are tattered rags, yet everybody is happy to share what they have, including food, except the Christians who steal the belongings of others. The kastom people refer to the Christians as thieves and liars. Natu gave me two beautiful, fine weave woollen shawls for Namu and Nahu. I have seen them worn in the evenings by many different women and girls when the temperature had fallen.

The Chief was meant to return to hospital in Lenakel to have his stitches removed three days ago but he still hasn't been yet. He went to the local health clinic at Loanengo village two days ago, but they were closed. His hand was swollen and his dressings were filthy although he had better mobility of his fingers.

I sat on the front doorstep of my leaf hut to take in the beauty of this wonderful place and to commune with Kassoso. I filled my lungs with the sweet air, laden with the perfume of tropical flowers. The sky was a brilliant blue in colour, with billowing white clouds forming directly over the volcano crater, drifting lazily away above the verdant tree canopies. Every plant was evergreen, so yellowing leaves dropped constantly throughout the year, which the girls raked up each morning at dawn around the village. The sun was shining and a pleasant cool breeze blew through my hut.

Many species of flowers bloomed in profusion, such as different coloured hibiscus, lilies and orchids, many I didn't recognise. A myriad of birds was busy feeding or flying, such as green and red parakeets, honeyeaters, silvereyes, martins and eagles. Dragonflies and butterflies, some large, others small, splashed their vivid bright colours amongst the red and green foliage, alighting on flowers to drink nectar. A small iridescent golden bronze lizard scuttled across the sun-baked ground into the shade beneath where I sat, casting an upwards glance towards me. Another lizard of the same size, which had an iridescent blue stripe down the centre of its olive green back, watched it pass from its vantage point of a hollowed tree stump. Yasur exploded occasionally, sending his sulphurous clouds, fire and fine black ash high into the air, which covered everything in glistening particles or black glass-like dust. Other eagles had joined the first to soar in the rising thermals.

Around the village were grown coconut, breadfruit, pawpaw, mango, banana, citrus, manioc, taro, water taro, yams, cabbage and kava, plus other fruits and vegetables. Bright yellow hornets and countless species of insect flew or crawled on virtually every surface. My daydreams were interrupted by a dog barking. Then a child cried. Two girls laughed in the distance. Men called to each other across the valley. Everything was pulsing with life, vitality and energy here. Energy flowed openly and free, not tightly constricted and sluggish such as in a city.

Nikwei called at my hut, presenting to me a large cup he had carved out of the soft yellow volcanic stone as a gift for Natu. He laughed and walked away. The Chief then called to take me to Donald's encampment to see the feast preparations for the nakamal tonight. Men were raking away hot volcanic stones from the fire embers with split poles to make an earth oven. The pig had been killed and butchered and lap lap made, which was wrapped in ferns and banana leaves. The lap lap was put on the hot embers, then the pig's head and one whole side of bacon, which was covered with more leaves, hot stones and soil. One of the girl helpers had a small wild grey tabby kitten on her shoulder. The kitten's mother had been killed to eat so the girl took the kitten as a pet, feeding it coconut milk that had been boiled to bring out the oil.

The Chief asked me to do some more healing on a very sick baby called Frankie, who I saw a few days ago. Frankie was Jack's son. He was clearly not well and had deteriorated since I last saw him. The baby was burning up with fever in the upper body and head, but icy cold in the legs and feet. He screamed the entire time. I attempted to run energy through his body to bring the heat down to his cold legs, but he didn't want anyone near him so struggled at every attempt to help him. I told the Chief he needed to go to hospital. His mother put a nipple in his mouth, which calmed him down, but then he was distracted by something and pulled away, causing a stream of warm milk to spill down her front and on to the ground. The Chief told her to put her titty away.

To remove all traces of food and manure, Glenda was washing the pig's intestines in a bucket of water, to fry later in oil to eat. I noticed one of Natu's expensive wraps impaled on a barbed wire clothes line to dry out in the sun.

Donald and I returned to Itabu for more questions and answers, as the Chief had to go off to see someone in another village. I asked Donald to explain more about kastom food.

'Wild pussycats are easy to catch. You open some coconuts and leave them on the ground. The wild pussycats love them. When you catch a wild pussycat, if you put it into a basket with raw coconut and salt, it will never leave you. Another way to tame a wild pussycat is to blow tobacco smoke up its nose. This calms it down. If a wild pussycat smells tinned fish and you throw it some, once it has eaten it, it will always stay around for more. This is good, as wild pussycats eat rats and lizards. As a wild pussycat is a native animal, a Chief has a kastom stone for it in his nakamal. Dogs do not have a kastom stone. They have been introduced here.

'There are also wild dogs and goats in the forest. When you heard the dog howling the same night Kassoso put his hand through your window, he was calling to a wild dog in the jungle. Different Chiefs have kastom stones for particular native creatures. The Chiefs near the sea have kastom stones in their nakamals for sharks, dugongs and turtles. A special leaf is rubbed between your hands, then placed on the kastom stone, to call in the Chief's Apu or principal animal spirit. The Chief who has the shark stone calls in red, black and white sharks. If a man wants to eat shark, he goes to that Chief who holds the spirit stone. The Chief called to his Apu shark, the biggest teacher shark, who comes in; then smaller sharks follow it in and one of those is caught.

'If a man wants to eat turtle, he contacts the Chief who holds the turtle spirit stone and asks him for a turtle. The Chief calls his Apu turtle and smaller ones follow it, so one of these can be caught. An exchange is then made for the turtle with a pig and kava. Turtle meat tastes like sweet chicken. This process applies with all native species, such as yam, breadfruit or anything else.

'As you know, Iarueri, the Chief holds the spirit stones for flying fox, banana, nabanga and pig. If a man wants to eat flying fox, he has to come to the Chief for one and exchanges a pig and kava. The flying fox is the Chief's Apu which, of course, is Kassoso. The Chief is my Apu. Apu is the Bislama name for Chief, Elder, Wise Person or Teacher. The name in our native language is Kaha. Sometimes, if flying fox is roosting in a small tree, we cut the tree down, then spear flying fox when they're on the ground. If you want to catch a wild chicken in the forest, another way of doing that, instead of building a cage, is to find where the chicken roosts at night by finding its droppings. At night, you light a dry palm frond as a torch so you can see what you are doing, then shoot the chicken with a bow and arrow, as it will roost very high on thin branches. The dogs will get it for you when it falls out of the tree.

'We also love to eat the large larvae or maggots of a type of moth. There are two types, one that is about five inches long, called peere, and the shorter maggot about two inches long, called pricene. The larvae live in a particular type of tree which they will eventually kill. When the tree is dead you cut it down and split open the wood with an axe to collect many maggots. We fry them in oil with curry powder and salt. Sometimes we roast them in the embers of the fire until they cook inside. You bite off the head, then squeeze the contents of the maggot into your mouth. They are very good to eat, Iarueri.

'We rarely eat wild goats and never eat the head or the hooves. They smell, so we leave them for the Christians to eat. There are no frogs in Tanna. If we need to cut a new path through the forest, we have to do a ceremony at the nakamal and kill a pig and drink kava to connect to the Spirit of the Forest to get permission to do this and where the path should go. If plenty of food has been cooked for a feast, then we play the tam tam to let everyone know in the area who is hungry that food is available for free at Itabu.'

I asked Donald about the problems with the water tank. He replied saying that, when the tank was first installed high in the mountain range in 2005, it didn't give enough gravity feed pressure, so it was carried back down the mountain and installed next to the holed tank at Itabu. When the sun had been shining on the water pipes, the water came out very hot in the shower, which was very pleasant. The water was back on for lunchtime.

I was called for lunch. Unfortunately, it was lap lap. I managed to force down a small portion, as it tastes disgusting. Fortunately, there was also a little rice and some pig meat.

As I waited for the call to go to the nakamal, I shamanically tuned into Kassoso as best I could. I found myself standing in the nakamal. Dragons had gathered, guarding the three principal entrances. At the Kassoso gate, where the spirit highway ends from the volcano, was a huge red dragon. At the usual entrance from Donald's encampment stood a medium sized black dragon and at the far entrance stood a smaller white dragon, all facing inwards. There was no dragon at the fourth entrance. I didn't understand what this signified.

The Chief sent a young girl to collect me for the nakamal, which was the first time he had done this. As she led me through the village, her girlfriends teased her. She giggled. At Donald's village, I was asked to do more healing on Frankie. He was rapidly getting worse. Whatever was wrong had only happened about five days ago. Frankie was burning up from the knee to the head but icy cold from his knee down. Before, it was the whole leg. I did what I could under the circumstances. We went on to the nakamal.

Several men were already preparing kava and had the fire going. More men and boys arrived, including Nikwei who had brought along Roy. He greeted me warmly. What little hair he had remaining was now completely white. In all, there were 21 males present. Word had got around that there was a feast at Itabu tonight. I sat next to Nikwei. He had a bad cough, but continued to smoke his pipe, spitting into the fire. A large bowl of steamed pig flesh from the earth oven, rice and lap lap were carried in to the nakamal. One man was assigned the task of collecting large leaves and to count out how many males were present to distribute the food equally on to each leaf plate.

The Chief and I were called to drink kava. We thanked Kassoso for their continued connection and asked for a visit for tonight. After offering our prayers, I sat in silence at the fire, then was taken back to the restaurant for my evening meal, which turned out to be tea, nature identical jam and dog biscuits. I was glad of another light meal but began to hallucinate about a full English breakfast! The food here is very monotonous and bland. After the heavy lunch of pork and lap lap I had eaten, I didn't need another large meal anyway.

Rain clouds began to sweep in from the coast, obliterating the clear night sky into total darkness. I prayed it would not rain tonight whilst we were in the leaf shelter. The Chief told me to wait for him as before and he would come for me when the village had fallen asleep. I wondered if the jam raiders would strike again tonight. I waited about four hours for the Chief. The tooth from which the filling had come out in Singapore was now giving me more pain and discomfort. I prayed I could get back home without having to see a dentist either in Port Vila or Singapore.

The Chief came for me about 9.45 pm. We made our way to the nakamal by torchlight. The glowing red embers of the fire in the nakamal flared into small dancing flames in the breeze after the kava ritual. The heavy clouds had dispersed to allow the light from the stars to bathe the forest in a subdued light. It had become much colder now compared to last night so there were fewer mosquitoes. We crawled into the shelter and settled down for the night. The Chief had the pink satin sheet all to himself as I had a warm sweatshirt on.

I had a rough idea of the window of opportunity that presented itself for us. Kassoso would only come around midnight, say from 11 pm to 1 am. They would not come at any other time. I estimated the time and knew we would move into that time slot very soon. We dozed off. As we moved into the critical time zone, the Chief began to snore so loudly that you could have heard him half a mile away. He coughed, moaned, whined, muttered in his sleep, spluttered, whimpered, tossed and turned, belched, farted and generally became a one-man zoo. I wanted to smack him on the back of the skull, but refrained from doing so. This uninterrupted loud noise lasted for the whole of the critical time period, magically easing into a light snooze after it had passed. I felt bitterly disappointed. Kassoso did not come.

15th October 2012:
Lake Isiwi   Spear in Head   Black Smoke

At first light I heard a bush rat chewing on a fallen coconut near to our shelter. We both crept out to urinate. I tripped over a concealed root which almost sent me sprawling into the bushes. We decided to return to the village as we both knew Kassoso would not come now.

For the first time I noticed what appeared to be the remains of a sunken grave at the edge of the nakamal near to our shelter. I made a mental note to enquire about this during our next session of questions and answers. We walked into Donald's encampment and were met by Namu carrying Frankie in her arms. He looked seriously ill. The Chief asked me to do more healing for the baby so I did what I could, praying to Spirit for help. I told the Chief again that the baby needed to see a doctor at the hospital. The Chief agreed, saying that he would take him to hospital today and would see about getting his stitches removed from his hand at the same time. I knew that local people avoid going to hospital because they have to pay for their medical treatment. Many do not have money so are dependent upon the kastom doctors for healing for an exchange of food or similar.

I asked the Chief to buy some bread and eggs for me at the market in Lenakel for a change, as I was struggling to eat the boring rice and dog biscuits given to me for most of my meals. The Chief looked surprised that I didn't like rice (the truth is – I have never liked rice). The Chief left to organise a truck to go to Lenakel. Of course, when the family heard of a chance to go to the main town on the island to go shopping, everybody vied for a place on the truck to get a day out from their monotonous routines. The fares for locals are very cheap and for non-locals very expensive.

I returned to my hut for 5 am. By 6.30 am the Chief and his party had left for Lenakel. I prayed to Kassoso that, in the six evenings that remained of my stay, we could make the appropriate contact. I thought for a long time about the situation last night. The very time that Kassoso would have come the Chief went into human zoo mode. After that critical time had passed, he slept comparatively quietly. I wondered if this was a message from Kassoso that they wanted to make the connection with me when I was alone.

I went to the toilet before breakfast but the last of the paper had been used by someone else. I was always prepared for this eventuality by carrying my own in my inner pocket. There was no water again to wash or drink. I knew that as soon as Donald realised this he would despatch more boys to clear out the silted pipes.

Donald arrived during my breakfast of exotic dog biscuits saying his father had told him to take me for a hike into the rain forest to show me kastom plants and places. By 8 am we were on the road. Donald took me to see the remains of the former Lake Isiwi which I had visited in 2004 with him. It had silted up after a violent storm in about 2003. Donald said the lake was good for fishing and washing and belongs to his father, but another man said it belonged to him, so he caused trouble. The Chief went to the sacred cyclone stone and did a ceremony to call down the Spirit of the Cyclone to fill the lake with stone and silt so nobody else could use it again. Donald said the Chief will keep the lake blocked until he decides to do another ceremony to the Spirit of the Cyclone to unblock and clear the lake, calling back the fish. Donald added that the water in the lake was warm from volcanic activity.

We continued along the track leading to Port Resolution. A large brown butterfly flew directly towards me, landing on my heart, then, after a few seconds, flew away. Donald thought this was a seriously good omen. I marvelled at the sacred dance of life. We watched eagles soaring in the rising thermals. A large yellow heart-shaped leaf glided down upon the breeze from one of the trees, landing at my feet. I watched it approach me as if a small boy had launched a paper dart.

We found wild raspberries at the edges of the road, which Donald said were called fembas. They were delicious. We left the road and passed into the rain forest. Donald cut open a couple of sprouting coconuts with his machete for us to eat. Once the coconut begins to germinate, the liquid (milk) inside becomes solid and oily and tastes like soap. As we walked along the forest trail, Donald pointed out wild kava and yam plants and other medicinal herbs. Donald stopped to point out to me a different species of banyan tree. He started to laugh, tears filling his eyes. Donald began telling me a story. He slapped the broad blade of his machete against his thigh, fighting back tears as he sniggered.

'Iarueri, when we were boys we used to practise with bows and arrows and throwing spears. One day, Jack, Enoch and I were having spear practice at a target. I threw my spear and missed so Jack ran to fetch it from behind the target, not realising that Enoch had already thrown his spear! I shouted to Jack to get out of the way but he didn't hear me. Enoch's spear hit Jack in the side of his head between his right eye and his ear. Jack fell to the ground screaming, blood pouring out of his head all over him and the ground. He cried for his mother and father to pull the lodged spear out of his head. Enoch was very frightened so ran off into the jungle, as he thought he had killed his brother. Jack lay on the ground crying so I went over to help him. I grabbed his hair with one hand and knelt on Jack's face with my knee and pulled the spear out of his head with my other hand. Blood poured out of the hole everywhere! The Chief was called and told so he sent me off to find Enoch and bring him home. After several days I finally found Enoch, with help from the dogs, asleep high up in a banyan tree, like this one. I climbed up and woke Enoch, who almost fell out of the tree with fright, telling him to come home. He refused as he still thought he had killed Jack and was afraid his father would kill him as punishment. I persuaded him that his brother was OK, so we returned back to Itabu. On our arrival home, the Chief told Enoch that he had to provide a chicken for Jack as payment, which he did. The matter was then resolved.'

Donald was bent over laughing. I told Donald about a similar story that happened to me, 'As boys my brother Barry and I made spears from long sticks. We stood some distance apart in a field throwing the spears at each other to see who was the bravest and didn't move. It was Barry's turn to throw his spear at me. I saw the spear coming for my face so moved out of the way, but stumbled reaching out with my hand to steady myself. In so doing, the spear stuck deeply into my hand, blood pouring out everywhere. Barry helped me back to the house where my mother pulled out the spear at the kitchen sink, at which point I fainted.'

Donald laughed. I showed him the scar in my right hand which I have carried for 50 years!

We made our way back to the nakamal at Itabu. I asked Donald about the grave-like holes in the ground. We stood at the edge of one which measured about five feet long by three feet wide, with a deep hole at one end. The "grave" had sunk about 18 inches. Donald pointed out several similar holes, especially one near to our leaf shelter. Donald said that they were not graves. He went on to explain that, when a large kastom dance was being performed in the nakamal, one man was stamping his feet in the usual manner when the ground gave way and he fell into a deep hole, breaking his leg. Donald told me to lie down on the ground and reach into the hole, which I did. It was extremely hot, venting volcanic fumes. Basically, the nakamal was a thin crust over a network of volcanic faults and magma. As the Chief's father, the former High Chief, is buried in the nakamal I presumed he would now be well cooked in what transpired to be a very large earth oven.

As we continued on to the village, Donald stopped to point out a type of plant that looked like a yucca but had white lily-like flowers which filled the air with a rich perfume, like jasmine. Donald explained that these plants are not found anywhere else as they are the kastom plant for the flying fox. He said they were called peep. We arrived back at my hut for 10 o'clock. At 10.15 am Nahu called me for lunch! Lunch was one whole cucumber, cut into thick rings, laid across a plastic plate. I had bought a small container of salt in Port Vila to keep my sodium levels up because of constant sweating, so I applied copious quantities to the cucumber. It was actually delicious, in fact one of the best meals Nahu had prepared! I fantasised about the Chief arriving back with fresh bread and eggs for dinner.

I returned to my hut to connect with Kassoso through shamanic dreaming.

I travelled to the realm of crystal and fire and experienced a long and detailed journey. Eventually I met again with the King of Kassoso who, on this occasion, wore a purple robe. Each time I return, I experience or see things in more detail; more is revealed. He was flanked, as before, by his nobles. I asked for permission to speak, which was granted.

'My brother, High Chief Wai Wai Rawi and I returned to the nakamal last night to connect to Kassoso but they never came.'

The King replied, 'You were not meant to connect last night. The agreement was for the night before. However, from now on, you must find your own way of communicating with us. The Chief has brought you to this point where first contact has been made. You have served each other well as brothers. It is time for you both to travel on individual paths now. You have been given the "keys" for this guidance. Remember these and keep to a strict discipline of connecting with us. We have heard your prayers asking for proof of authenticity. We understand the reasons you requested this and in council it has been agreed to allow you to experience certain phenomena rarely given to those on, shall I say, the wrong side of the veil (laughter). You will have your wish, my brother, and you will receive the appropriate gifts from us in due course, when the time is right and not before. Go now.'

'May I ask a question, please?'

'Yes.'

'Why do Kassoso only manifest around midnight in the physical world?'

'It is the time of least resistance, a time when everything human, in the kastom world anyway, is still, when the vapours of the heart-felt prayers can reach our shores. It is a time of inner poise for communication. We move about silently in the shadows, for, if we revealed our true nature and identity to humanity as we have done in the past, we would be persecuted and men would try to hunt and kill us through fear and ignorance due to generations of false dogma and indoctrination by those who once communicated and worked with us, but who wanted to keep this knowledge and power for themselves. Their "truth" was reversed so that our race became demonised, classed as evil beings from hell.'

I thanked the King. As I looked around me, I noticed dragons moving silently through the surrounding landscape watching us, breathing black smoke. Iridescent fungi illuminated caves and recesses similar to those that are found in the undisturbed rain forest today. After further detailed encounters, my guides and I returned and I reintegrated back into my physical body.

One of the things that I remembered clearly, as I wrote up this vision in my journal, was that the dragons were breathing black smoke. I recalled a bizarre experience I had in 2011. Maggie and I were having breakfast together at home, enjoying each other's company and chatting over hot tea. Suddenly, as I was speaking, black smoke, or a smoke-like vapour, poured out of my mouth engulfing my face and head. I couldn't see Maggie physically for a few seconds. When it cleared, I could tell by Maggie's expression, wide eyes and open mouth, that she had witnessed a materialisation from a different dimension. She was freaked out and clearly afraid. To date, I still have no idea what that phenomenon was nor have I heard of anyone else experiencing it. I was glad that Maggie was a witness to it. The same thing occurred later in the day but not as powerfully and has never occurred since, at least not to my knowledge. Who knows what happens in the darkness or when you sleep!

I sat on the step of my leaf hut waiting for the call to go to the nakamal. Above my head in the thatch several leaf-cutting bees arrived carrying rolled up pieces of green leaf, rather like a sleeping mat, one at a time, disappearing into a dried curled piece of palm leaf. They must have been building a hive of some sort. They made many journeys until the last leaf wouldn't fit, so they cut it off and it fell to the ground. On a piece of wood I noticed a small hairy caterpillar with a yellow head. Its body was all white at the front and all black at the back. Then a black and white butterfly flew past me which had delicate tints of orange and blue upon its wings. I thought it fascinating, with the myths of the black and white serpents, that so many creatures in nature here were black and white, including the sea snakes and the mosquitoes.

I tied up my mosquito net over the bed in the hope that Kassoso would reach for me through the open window again during the night or walk into my hut through the open door. I was prepared for them.

The Chief's party arrived back from Lenakel at 5 pm. Donald came for me later to take me to the nakamal. He had shaved off his beard. I hardly recognised him, he looked so different; in fact, just like a younger version of his father. I asked him why he had shaved off his beard, as it is a symbol of high grade in this part of the island.

'Iarueri, I have done this to honour my father and you for speaking with Kassoso.'

I asked Donald what happened with Frankie at hospital. He replied that he had been kept in overnight for observation because the doctors didn't know what was wrong with him. 'Maybe he will come home tomorrow.' he said.

We arrived at the nakamal. There were 15 males present. I sat next to the Chief, who asked me what dreams or visions I had had last night or through the day with Kassoso. I told him I experienced nothing in the shelter last night. I didn't say why. The Chief said he heard them walking about around the shelter, making noises like an animal. The Chief told me that they knew my smell now, so will come. I told him about the vision I had where Kassoso had told me that we both had to make the connection alone, so there was no need to sleep in the shelter tonight. The Chief disagreed with me, telling me that we would return to the shelter tonight to speak with Kassoso. I had no option but to go along with the Chief's decision and had to trust that it was right.

A youth passed through the nakamal, hobbling painfully with the aid of a heavy staff. One of the other men said to me that he was playing football and went over on his ankle, snapping his strings (ligaments). The man said that he will see the kastom doctor tomorrow, who will cut him to the bone to get rid of the bad blood. The Chief still hadn't had the stitches removed from his hand for some reason. He said he would have them taken out tomorrow.

After the kava ritual, I was escorted back to the restaurant for a meal of fresh bread and fried eggs. Sadly, the fried eggs were cold and saturated in old cooking oil. Several eggs were mangled and piled high in the centre of the plate. I struggled to eat them. When Natu and I were at Itabu in 2010, Natu went to a lot of trouble to teach Nahu how to cook eggs and how to check if an egg was stale or fresh by floating it in water. If it floated, it was full of gas and bad; if it sank, it was edible. She taught Nahu how to make an omelette and other things, such as checking use by dates on tins, which they were unaware about. Natu also taught Nahu about personal hygiene and how to maintain a hygienic kitchen. Obviously, none of this information had had any effect. The girl really has no idea how to prepare a meal. Eggs are rarely eaten in Itabu, as the pigs or dogs eat them in the jungle when found and they are expensive to buy, so are seen as a luxury.

The Chief called for me at 10 pm. We went to the nakamal, crawling in to the leaf shelter to settle down to sleep. The night sky was clear and sparkling with starlight. Flying foxes foraged in the nearby branches for fruit to eat, calling to each other. The humid night air was heavy with the intoxicating perfume of hoya flowers. A solitary firefly raced around the nakamal for several laps, as if his companion was timing him with a stopwatch. Wisps of smoke rose from the dying embers of the sacred fire. I love the smell of wood smoke.

Again, I could gauge the critical time when Kassoso would most likely come to make contact. The Chief slept peacefully and quietly, so all was well. I settled down to sleep; then as the time approached for Kassoso to come, the Chief went into human zoo mode again. He snored loudly and had several guttural coughing fits, by the sound of it, bringing up copious quantities of thick phlegm, chewing it with an open mouth then swallowing it noisily. Maybe it was another way to get a nicotine or kava fix! Anyway, it seriously turned my stomach, so I spent most of the night staring up at the stars through the leaf shelter and listening to the flying foxes crying overhead, dropping twigs on to our shelter. The Chief stopped snoring and chewing his phlegm snacks two hours later; then fell silently asleep.

Kassoso did not come, as predicted. I tried to turn my frustration and annoyance into a positive mindset by just enjoying the opportunity to sleep in the rain forest under a canopy of stars, including the Southern Cross constellation, and listening to the amazing sounds of the jungle at night.

16th October 2012:
Burial ritual   Opening tombs   Death and Dying Yasur volcano

We both got up at first light, probably at 4.30 am. The Chief disappeared so I wandered about the nakamal to enjoy the fresh new day. A couple of large black pigs foraged nearby in the undergrowth then found the remnants of the kava roots by the nakamal fire and ate those. Pigs will eat anything, including human excrement. A small child began to sing nearby. The village was stirring.

I glanced at the banyan tree and the secret spirit stones in its shadow. I saw a pair of large white eyes staring at me! As my eyes adjusted to the dim light, I saw a small boy squatting on his haunches wearing only a pair of ragged shorts. He was clearly wondering what this hairy white alien was doing in his patch. I waved to him. He looked confused then ran off. Soon afterwards a man and an older boy arrived. I waved to them, as I imagined I would be the last thing they would expect to see in the nakamal at this time of day. The man returned the greeting and came over to speak to me. He spoke good English, so I took the opportunity to ask him questions about the kastom tradition. He spoke clearly and with ease. I asked him to explain to me about the funerary rites or rituals of the kastom people in this part of Tanna Island, as every area has different practices.

'When someone dies, the body is dressed in their good clothes and wrapped in several blankets or sheets, then bound inside several pandanus mats, all tied up tightly with rope into a bundle before the body is put into a deep hole in the ground, head down first. This is to stop the pigs from digging up the corpse to eat it. Nobody in the family works for three days during that time. Then we all meet up together for a feast. When a Big Chief dies, it is the same procedure, but only a Chief can be buried in the nakamal, as it is a sacred place. The feasting for a Big Chief is different. A bullock and many pigs are killed and kava is prepared. Chiefs, Elders and many people come from all over the island for the ceremony. The next Big Chief who will take over gathers everyone together and tells them what will happen under his rule. A month is allowed for mourning for a Big Chief.'

This reminded me about the two famadihana ceremonies that I was invited to participate in when I was in Madagascar by Chiefs Ranaivoandre and Razafimamonjisoa. After many years, their sacred tombs were opened and the bound and wrapped corpses carried out to enable their families to dance, sing and feast with them (See Appendix C).

Death and dying are very important issues for tribal peoples, indeed for all of us. As a shamanic practitioner, most of my work is orientated around this aspect. When somebody dies, their body can only be disposed of through one of the four elements, ie earth, air, fire or water. What happens to their spirit or soul? From my perspective, there is much confusion between the terms spirit and soul. As I understand it, your spirit is the divine spark that is and always will be unblemished and returns to its rightful place in the universe, wherever that is. This can reincarnate into another physical body or progress to a higher spiritual dimension, where physicality no longer exists, as there are many levels and overtones within each dimension.

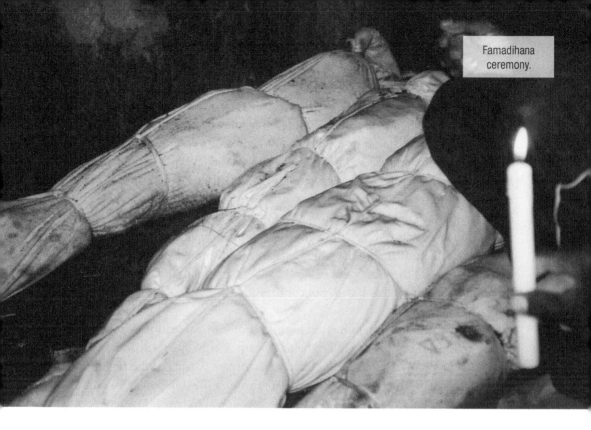

Famadihana ceremony.

The soul, however, is what we principally work with, as we are multi-dimensional beings. We have, depending on our belief systems, multiple souls, or a principal soul that can fragment or hive off into multiple parts. During trauma a soul part can separate and get lost during the dying process, usually becoming trapped in the lower astral dimensions or move into an overtone of another. The key to understanding this process and locating, releasing and healing lost soul parts is by working with the belief system, usually religious, of the individual concerned, but the same process can be used to work with the collective soul consciousness of families, clans, tribes and nations, along with their associated Gods, Goddesses, archetypes and ancestors.

If, at death, a person believes they will go to meet their ancestors in their ancient meeting halls or to their sacred tribal lands, this is what will occur. If a Christian believes that, when they die, an angel will take them to heaven, this will happen to the perceived belief of what heaven is to them. Likewise, if a person has been indoctrinated through religious propaganda and dogma that they are a vile sinner and will go to purgatory, hell and damnation, they will most probably go to such a place, because we are all co-creators and therefore have the ability to literally create our reality. We also have the ability to be co-destroyers. This is our personal free will choice in third dimensional reality. We then face the consequences of our actions, good and not so good, during the death process by judging ourselves.

What if an individual has no belief system? Where does their soul go at death? Do they stay in the environment of where they died, eg hospital, battlefield, road traffic accident, old people's home? Even though they may not have a belief system, they still have attending ancestors and spirit allies who will come to them to take them home. Some lost soul parts remain in the lower astral levels and come back in to attach to the energy body of other people. These souls are generally referred to as entities, but in truth they are suffering souls, because they are lost, afraid, confused and lonely. They come to us for help. When you talk about entities, demons, possession, exorcism, etc you draw this type of phenomenon to you. This is one reason why the fundamentalist Christians are so fearful of evil and demons. It is because that is all they think about, so the universe provides what they focus upon. Their cult doctrine is fear based, not compassionate.

Possession is a natural phenomenon in third dimensional reality, although it is not desirable. Possession is a major belief system of tribal peoples, so they need ceremony or ritual to be performed to give them safe passage at the time of death. The shaman helps the freed soul to navigate through the different sub-realms of their culture to their desired destination. Possession simply means we have other souls or beings within our personal sacred sovereign space. We are all "possessed" but, as long as these suffering souls do not start to control their host, we do not notice them and they leave when we keep our frequency high and our boundaries intact (maintaining personal boundaries is not the same as protection).

Most people in the West do not realise that the funeral ritual is not for the mourners' benefit but for the deceased. It is a ceremony to let the deceased know that they are actually dead and it gives them permission to detach and leave. Sadly, a lot of people in the West are so drugged by the medical profession, at the time of their death, they move into a state of limbo, which is cruel. Because of the effects of these drugs, sometimes they mistake angels for demons and refuse to leave the environment they died in, often latching on to family members, strangers or even objects.

A good death is when a person has clarity of their senses and sacred space is held around them so they experience a beautiful tranquil passing. Their ancestors or spirit allies come to meet them immediately at death, but they should not linger too long in this temporary environment but be encouraged through prayers and ceremony to go straight on to their correct destination, wherever that is. This prepares them for their next role or incarnation.

Just because a soul passes into the spirit world does not mean that it automatically becomes enlightened or spiritually aware. Spirits need educating and usually need a lot of healing after death, especially if the death was traumatic, before they can move on to higher spheres. Most of the church rituals and ceremonies were taken and then altered from their original "Earth based" traditions, so fracturing the true energetic connections to the ancient tribal lineage keepers. These ceremonies became incomplete and had the effect of closing down the third eye during baptism and trapping soul parts of the dead through giving the "last rites". A ceremony can be done to reverse these misguided practices.

I have permission to reveal a story regarding a funerary ritual. We have to take care that some spiritual experiences are to remain secret. Some can be told.

Since I was a boy I have always wanted to be a priest or an undertaker. To my childish mind, they were one and the same anyway.

A few years ago I was offered a position as a trainee Funeral Director with a local firm. After training for about six months I had an amazing spiritual experience.

Manannan came to me during a shamanic journey and told me that I was to perform a funerary ritual for a Mer Child. It was not a request. Manannan drew me into the sea and placed me behind him astride his sacred white horse Enbarr, who took us into the dark depths of the ocean, escorted by Mer Men, to a secret submarine cavern system. Its entrance was guarded night and day by the Mer warriors. It was a holy place for this race.

We passed the guards and entered into a huge circular domed crypt containing countless recesses, rather like honeycomb, which held their dead. Manannan introduced me to a small gathering of Mer Folk, including the bereaved family who had lost their small child through tragic circumstances, a rare occurrence by all accounts.

I performed the funeral ceremony for the child and its body was interred within the family crypt. It was a huge privilege and a remarkable and emotional experience. I came out of meditation and realised, without any doubt, that I had fulfilled my desired role as a Funeral Director and had no further need to remain in this profession. I resigned and returned to my shamanic practice.

The lesson I learned through this experience was that there is a right time to fulfil a sacred task but the skill is recognising the call and to have the courage to follow your heart by trusting in Spirit.

Mount Yasur
Volcano.

I went for breakfast. Nahu had once again destroyed a good meal! I had fried eggs which were cold and dripping in old oil. I struggled to eat the mountain of mush on my plate, eating as much dry bread as I could to soak up the fat. As was often the case, the only piece of cutlery Nahu had left out for me was a small teaspoon!

The Chief arrived for some questions and answers. I drew sketches in my journal of both of my tribal tattoos and asked the Chief to explain to me what they meant. This he did (see Appendix D). The Chief asked if I wanted to go to Yasur volcano, so I said I would love to do that again. He arranged for Donald to take me later on. Even though I had been there many times before, I always had to have an escort in case I fell into the crater and got fried, grilled, steamed, baked or roasted.

I saw the man who I spoke to in the nakamal at dawn. He told me that one of Donald's children was sick so Melissa would take me to the volcano instead. At 7.30 am Melissa called for me. She was a slim girl about 15 years old and had put on her best clothes for this occasion. She had large soft brown eyes with the most amazing eyelashes, the sort you see on camels. Melissa asked me to wait by the restaurant whilst she disappeared, returning soon afterwards with her friend Hannay and a small boy called Peter. I guessed Hannay was the same age as Melissa and Peter about 10 years old. The girls whispered and giggled between themselves for most of the journey; Peter was very serious, frowning constantly. He clearly felt he was responsible for the safety of the white man. He seemed to carry the weight of the world on his young shoulders.

When we met the girls' friends along the road, they all giggled and wanted to know what heinous crime they had committed to earn the punishment of escorting the white man. We passed a cleared piece of land that was used as a football pitch. Two sets of goal posts had been cut from the jungle, which were basically small trimmed trees. All four goalposts were sprouting leaves! Everything grows with ease in this rich volcanic soil.

We arrived at the tourist tollgate at the bottom of the volcano but nobody was there to take my payment. Melissa was obviously distressed about this so I assured her I would pay on my return. Another small boy joined our party, which clearly pleased Peter. The girls giggled, the boys chased about making a noise. I wanted to pay my respects to Yasur in a prayerful state and in silence so I decided to put my hiking boots into four-wheel drive. The heat and humidity transformed into a light fine drizzle, which soon became gentle rain. Melissa carried an umbrella for such an eventuality but I declined to use it as I wasn't a tourist but an honorary member of the tribe. Melissa and the other children understood and smiled with acknowledgment.

Since my last visit the road had been widened and several gangs of men were working to fill in holes and repair eroded sections of the track. I was fascinated at the volcanic vents that spewed out hot gases and white steam along the length of the road. Ferns and mosses seemed to thrive in this primeval environment. The track soon became steep as we climbed higher. I got myself into a steady walking pace, maintaining my stamina by breathing in a controlled way. Melissa wanted to know if I needed a rest. I didn't. She and her companions fell silent, trailing behind me. I had the peace I needed to communicate with Kassoso and Yasur. I was saturated with sweat, my shirt stuck to my back. I also had indigestion from Nahu's greasy eggs.

We reached the base of the last push to the crater rim. Somebody had built a concrete path since my last visit to help the bloated tourists who usually came up in a four-wheel drive truck. We got to the crater rim but, because of the low rain cloud, we couldn't see into the crater itself. As the cloud and fumes came and went, I noticed that a huge section of the inner crater had collapsed within itself and there was lots of erosion. I got the impression that a big explosion was building for an eruption. The strong wind along with rain was very cold. The loud explosions within the crater frightened the children, causing the girls to scream each time. They didn't want to go any further. They were miserable in the exposed environment and bad weather.

It became dangerous because we couldn't see where the falling lava bombs were landing due to the low cloud so we decided to return to Itabu. The girls were concerned that their skirts were blowing up in the wind so they kept twisting and turning and had to hold down their skirts with both hands. I have often seen the older women's legs when the wind blew open their skirts to reveal many types of tribal tattoos.

The children were much quieter on our return journey. We passed one work gang where the men were all lying in the hedge smoking. I recognised the only person who was standing as Chief Tukuriary. He was always dignified with a huge black and white beard. Thankfully, I remembered his name and greeted him, bowing slightly. He was quite taken aback at my recognising him as he obviously remembered me. The other men were impressed with my kastom protocol, so all stood to honour me.

We arrived at the tollgate so I offered to pay my fee to the female attendant but she had no change at all, so ended up by keeping the higher denomination note. The boy who joined us ran off. When we were about half a mile from Itabu the heavens opened and it poured down. Puddles soon formed in the road with the deluge. One young man, who wore nothing more than a tattered pair of red shorts, lay in one of the puddles in the middle of the road singing! A couple of men passed carrying rifles, a huge status symbol in these parts.

Melissa and I decided to share the umbrella; the other two got soaked. By the time we had reached the village the rain had stopped. It was 10 am. I asked Melissa what I owed her for being my guide but she didn't know. I told her I would speak to the Chief about it later. If she provided a service, then she gets paid for it. I think it is important to encourage children. That was my tenth visit to Yasur volcano.

At 11.15 am I was called for lunch. Nahu had cremated more fried eggs, along with some manioc. I managed to get the eggs down but couldn't face the manioc. I tried telling Nahu that I didn't want eggs for every meal, just for a change, but she didn't understand.

After lunch I had a shower, the first proper wash for three days as the water pipes were blocked. The water had come directly off the mountain so was icy cold, as it hadn't had time to heat up in the pipes lying in the ground. I also did some laundry.

A truck arrived and the Chief and Donald got out, along with others. Jack's baby Frankie is still in hospital under observation and the Chief had his stitches removed from his hand. He was given medication but will not use it. Donald took his sick child to the hospital but it appeared to be fine now. I never found out which child it was or what the trouble was.

I returned to my hut to connect with Kassoso but found it difficult as I was very cold. I craved for a hot cup of tea! I made a connection with Kassoso and, as I was finishing, a dog started to howl in an eerie way as it did on the night that the Kassoso hand came through my window.

As I waited for Donald to come to escort me to the nakamal, I strolled around the village. The first white and purple passion fruit flowers had opened. There was a place near the restaurant where rubbish, such as plastics and tins, were thrown. Occasionally, it is burnt. I felt sad that this rubbish would be there for generations to come. Donald came for me at 5 pm. He said the Chief was visiting Glenda in Sergay village so would drink kava there. It appears to be good protocol for the High Chief to drink kava in the nakamals of the other Chiefs under his rule. There were only four men at the nakamal tonight. I asked Donald to tell Nahu that I only wanted tea and dog biscuits for dinner, as I still felt unwell after all of those greasy eggs.

After the kava ritual, I went back to the restaurant for my dinner, which was more greasy fried eggs, a cucumber and a tomato. Dog biscuits and tea were included. I had had ten or more fried eggs in three consecutive meals. I was constipated; I felt like a pregnant dodo. I have found over my many stays at Itabu that my biggest tests and trials were taking kava and tackling the inedible food. I usually lost a lot of weight when I was with the tribe.

It was exceptionally windy tonight. The curtains blew horizontally in my hut, which was good to keep the mosquitoes away, although I did get bitten a few times. Malaria is found in the northern islands of Vanuatu but rarely in the southern islands. Kava is believed to kill the malarial parasites by the kastom people, yet the women are not permitted to drink it. I prayed to Kassoso to come to me during the night.

17th October 2012:
Kitchen House on Fire   Fish Ritual
Hostel for Homeless Men

Kassoso did not come to me during the night, or at least not in a way I noticed. I felt bitterly disappointed; in fact, I felt bereft at missing another opportunity so fragile and rare. I felt it was really important that I was to make a physical connection with Kassoso whilst I was in Itabu, their homeland, where their secret spirit stone is. I told myself not to lose hope and to keep thinking positively.

I went for breakfast and found a new jar of Pakistan nature identical flavoured mango jam, along with dog biscuits and tea. The Chief arrived for our morning questions and answers session. He showed me his hand where the stitches had been removed yesterday. The swelling had gone down considerably so he could move his fingers a little now. I noticed clean dressings on his wounds, including the wound made by the kastom doctor.

Somehow our discussion got on to fire. The Chief went into great detail about how Donald's kitchen house had burnt down in a storm, describing the inferno, the women and children screaming and the men trying to beat back the flames to prevent the fire spreading to other nearby leaf huts. Others tried to salvage the few meagre items the family possessed. This was the third time this story had "crossed my path", which indicated to me that Spirit needed me to pay attention to what this lesson was about, or to allow myself to move into the emotion the Chief was experiencing as he related this dramatic story.

I moved into a state of receptivity and resonance with the Chief until I became anxious myself, feeling his fear and helplessness. Interestingly, at that point, I moved into my own drama of an unpleasant experience that had been buried over the years and was now surfacing again. The Chief's story rekindled frightening memories of when our estranged father threatened to come to our house in the middle of the night to burn our family alive by pouring petrol through the letter box then lighting it. I knew it wasn't an idle threat; he meant it. I spent several sleepless nights waiting for him to come, remaining fully dressed with my boots still on, with a forester's axe at the side of my bed to protect my family if the need arose. When I informed the authorities about my father's credible threats, none were interested and said, 'We cannot intervene until he actually does it.'

It would have been too late then! I told the Chief my story which enabled me to release the tension around it. He was clearly upset. I felt tired. The Chief said that wherever there was fire, there was Kassoso.

'Iarueri, I spoke to Kassoso in a dream last night and they want you to hold their stick of power. They are hesitant to come back, as they had presented their staff before. They said it wasn't their problem that a plastic mosquito net got in the way.'

The Chief said that we could try rolling back the mosquito net then, if the mosquitoes were too bad, roll it back down again. We would go to the nakamal tonight. I asked the Chief if one of the other Chiefs held the spirit stone for the mosquito and, if so, could ceremony be done to keep them away until we had made contact with Kassoso. For some reason, the Chief avoided answering this question but added that mosquitoes are only a problem if a village is not clean. I presumed he meant all of the fallen or discarded coconut shells that fill with rain water for the mosquitoes to breed in.

'Iarueri, I will ask Kassoso what time they will come tonight so we can be prepared and ready. When Kassoso are in the air, they are flying fox. When they are on the ground, they become secret men – the Dragon Men after eating pig and drinking kava.'

The Chief looked at me directly into my eyes, almost trance-like, then spoke again, 'Iarueri, Kassoso say they will come to you in Manannan's Island if the right road is made. To do this, you must do ceremony in your nakamal. You can use a black chicken or a fish, but the fish must come straight from the sea at about 3 to 4 pm, not in the morning when it can go bad in the sun, and not tinned or from an ice box. One of the symbols of Majikjiki is the fish when that was all he and his family had to eat when they were adrift on the open seas. You must make the ceremony at dusk by lighting a fire in your nakamal and cook the fish over the fire like we do in the nakamal at Itabu. You must not use oil and you must not use sheep, bullock or anything else. You take the head of the fish and talk to him so that his spirit makes a clear road to Kassoso here. Position the fish to face Yasur volcano, then call to Tangarua and Majikjiki to help you to connect to Kassoso. Give the fish head to Kassoso by burying it at the base of a tree somewhere that a dog cannot find it. A flying fish is best. We call these the "chicken of the sea", or in our language Ban Kassoso.'

I explained to the Chief that we do not have flying fish in the seas around the Isle of Man. He said an ordinary fish is fine, adding that, if you don't get an answer or a visit from Kassoso, you keep on trying.

'Iarueri, when we kill pig or chicken, the blood goes into the ground for the spirit to go straight to Kassoso. When the Kassoso arm came through your window, you felt no power when you held the hand because we had not done this ceremony first. If Kassoso do not like you and do not want you in their home, they will try to kill you or they could make you very sick. My brother, I need to buy a chicken and kava for tonight to talk to Kassoso. They need to know that you have provided these for them.'

I gave the Chief the necessary money and he left immediately to go to the market. He said he would be back about 2 pm so wanted me to connect with Kassoso in my hut.

Strong winds developed and it began to rain again. I prayed that the weather would be favourable for our stay in the leaf shelter at the nakamal. I also prayed that the Chief would not go into human zoo mode again. I did a shamanic journey to meet with Kassoso and found everything harmonious and encouraging. I looked forward to tonight with anticipation and joy. I felt ready!

I was called for lunch at 10.30 am by Nahu. It was another meal of cold greasy mangled fried eggs with one tomato. I struggled to get the food down. I soon realised why lunch was so early, as three beautifully dressed Ni-Van matriarchs had just arrived at Itabu by truck escorted by Nahu. They walked to Donald's village. I wondered why there was a frenzied clean-up prior to their arrival.

The rain had given way to showers, then bright and sunny skies. As usual, the wet earth and huts steamed from the heat of the sun. I sat on the step of my leaf hut to enjoy the beauty of nature around me. I noticed a small black and white spider constructing its web, so fine you couldn't see it. It appeared that she was doing a circular dance in mid-air between two plants. Occasionally the wind blew her, so she stopped her weaving and remained still until the breeze had passed, continuing in her secret domain. A species of hibiscus had flowers that hung like scarlet bells against the green foliage. A different species had huge yellow flowers that gazed up at the sun. The flowers changed every couple of days. There was always something different to see.

At about 3 pm, the three matriarchs left the village. Laughter and shouting resumed as normal. I don't know who these women were but, during their visit, the village was totally silent. The clouds became thicker and showers started again as the wind became stronger. As I waited for the call to go to the nakamal, I noticed a mynah bird struggling to fly with a large piece of yellow plastic held in its beak. It dropped it. This was the second time I had seen these birds flying with large pieces of plastic, perhaps to construct nests with.

The Chief called for me at 5 pm to go to the nakamal. At Donald's village, I was asked to do some healing on a young man called Nassey who had a chest problem. He had got drunk one night and was involved in a fight where he was hit violently in the chest. This injury prevented him from doing any heavy work. After I had finished doing some energy work with him, he said to me, 'I could feel your power, Iarueri. I will bring my lady to see you tomorrow, who has a pain also.'

We arrived at the nakamal to find ten males present, including Chief Nogwaren and Chief Kiabi. Chief Nogwaren was very excited as he told me that Chief Wai Wai was going to give him one of the smoking pipes and tobacco I had brought for the men. Nassey wanted to prepare the kava for me to drink. This is considered a great honour if a man offers to do this. I bowed respectfully to acknowledge his gift in return for the healing. Kastom people cannot be obligated to anyone; there has to be an exchange of some sort, otherwise a man loses his power. A pot was brought into the nakamal by a small boy, which I guessed contained the chicken I had paid for.

The Chiefs and I sat on logs around the sacred fire as the boys and young men prepared the kava. Chief Kiabi turned to me and said, 'Iarueri, can you tell us why the Christians hate the kastom people so much?'

This was a topic brought up constantly, so I wasn't surprised by the question.

'My brother, I do not know the answer to this question. In all religions you will get good and bad people, as you will in the kastom traditions. In the past the mentality of many Christians towards the kastom peoples in the world generally was to convert (brainwash) them to their belief system of hellfire and damnation so they could control them through fear. Those who would not conform to these lies were tortured, as pain and screaming was seen as repentance, or killed. I think the reason the Christians hate the kastom peoples so much is that they are afraid of your power and your strong connection with God. They are jealous of your joy, love and freedom that God has bestowed upon you, whereas the Christians can be constrained, miserable and fearful. If you follow a spiritual path of truth, you live with joy and abundance.'

Chief Kiabi drew deeply on a pipe the Chief had filled and lit for him, nodding as he stared into the fire. Another man raised his hand for permission to speak, 'Apu. What do you believe is true about the Church and Christians?'

The Chief sniggered. I was convinced he had set me up to face difficult questions tonight. 'My brother, with what I have read, there are over 900 different versions of the Bible. When these texts are translated and interpreted from originals, the person writing the new story always adds or removes information that he either does not understand or disagrees with, then he includes his personal beliefs and prejudices. These stories were changed time and again over the years until they no longer bear much truth or resemblance to the original works. The Church has been built upon these lies and, if you believe that there was such a person as Jesus, I am sure his teachings were based upon love, forgiveness, peace and compassion, which some Churches have little idea about. Remember, Jesus was a Rabbi, a Jewish priest. Christianity is, therefore, a Jewish cult. The different types of Christianity, you could say, are sub-cults, such as the Seventh Day Adventists.'

With the mention of the Seventh Day Adventists, most of the men coughed and spat on the ground with disgust. The Chief interrupted me. Everybody looked at me. I was under some pressure now.

'Iarueri, the boy asked you what you believed.' He sniggered again.

I thought to myself, if cannibalism had not been illegal, he would be roasting on a spit right now.

'My brother, my personal beliefs are not what other men believe, as it is simply my version of the truth. No man has all of the truth, because what we believe to be true is always our limitation.'

The Chief secretly kicked me on the leg and nodded to me, as much as to say, 'Keep going, you are not getting away with this one.' He sniggered again. I imagined him now trussed and bound along with roasted parsnips, pumpkin and potatoes, with my knife and fork at the ready!

I didn't know what to say, because my beliefs are personal to me and not necessarily for public airing. I tried to worm my way out of answering this question but the men wanted to know. I looked around me from where I sat. I was next to the sacred fire, beneath the sacred nabanga in the sacred temple. This was a holy place where I could not tell untruths. I was obligated to speak my truth. The Chief kicked me again. Chief Nogwaren sniggered this time. One of the men who could understand English spoke softly in Bislama to interpret to the others.

'My brothers, what I have personally found is that, as a general rule, whatever the Christians say, if you look at the opposite, you will get an idea of what is actually true. They do not want you and I, the kastom people, knowing the secrets and connecting to God directly. Have you all heard of Mary Magdalene?'

There was a bit of discussion around this as most men had heard, but some hadn't. After the men settled, I paused and drew breath.

'The Church made Mary out to be a bad person. In fact, she is the key to the true secret. I personally believe that Mary Magdalene was a high ranking Avatar, that is a Big Woman or Chief, someone with the same power as Majikjiki. She held the secret blood lineage and the power of God, as if she was the firstborn of Tangarua. To continue her sacred blood lineage of the God line, she needed to marry a man of an equal grade, or similar, to keep the lineage as pure as possible. Jesus was this man, who became Mary's husband and then they had children. Jesus was Mary's consort to continue to keep the female blood line holy.'

The men talked amongst themselves for a while. I think I had just stretched their possibilities for change. A man, who sat in the background, spoke softly, 'Apu. May I ask please – what is compassion?'

I looked at the man who had spoken. My heart went out to him, as he was dressed in rags. How do you answer such a question in a way he can understand?

'I will tell you a story and give you two examples.'

Everybody drew closer; someone coughed; Nassey came over to listen.

'In 2000 I went back to Australia, as I was drawn to go to a place called Mt Isa, a city in north-west Queensland. Somehow I became friendly with the Captain of the Salvation Army, another Christian cult, who invited me to his house and to the many functions and events that were on offer. He was a very good man, a man who was genuinely compassionate. This meant that he went out of his way, day and night, to help people who were in trouble, without reward or fame. I was trying to get a job at the time and eventually got a position on an isolated cattle station that was one million acres in size.

'I bought a return air ticket and flew to the remote town of Birdsville, where I was met by my employer who turned out to be a sadistic bully. His treatment towards me left me feeling humiliated, helpless, stupid and worthless. He gave me many dirty jobs to do, such as scraping up congealed blood clots and fat from under the meat house racks, which meant, to do this, I had to be on my hands and knees in this bloody mess. The stench was sickening in the heat. He took me and a couple of others to a boundary fence of a neighbour and killed one of his cattle, not one of his own, cutting off the beast's ears so it couldn't be identified by its owner's marks to see my reaction, presenting to me the bloody souvenirs. He laughed. My spirit was broken within seven days. I told him I wanted to leave. After more tormenting and ridicule, he took me back to the airport, where, thank God, I had a return ticket back to Mt Isa. I had no money, except some loose change, no job and nowhere to stay.

'I arrived back in Mt Isa and, with my remaining change, telephoned the Salvation Army Captain. He was at my side within 15 minutes. As we drove back into town, I burst into tears. I felt a complete failure and totally useless. I was now officially destitute he said. He comforted me and drove me to a local hostel for homeless men where he signed me in, paying for my upkeep through his church. All of my possessions were confiscated, including my watch and toothbrush. I was allowed nothing, except the clothes I stood up in. A series of inner gates were unlocked by guards and I was escorted to a dormitory where I was given one of the spare beds to sleep in. I was in prison! I felt wretched, afraid and alone, yet somehow I knew God was still with me.

'The following day I was given the job of cleaning out the latrines, whilst the other inmates had other duties, but all stared at me menacingly. After I had finished my chores, I was permitted out for a few hours to look for work but had to be back at the hostel by a certain time for curfew. I returned at the stated hour. I was escorted through the gates, which were locked behind me. I realised that to survive in this environment I had to interact with the other inmates, so I sat in the communal room to watch TV with the others, but they ignored me, except for one man who came up to me and introduced himself. He said that he had been watching me closely and said that the other men were wary of me because I was too clean and smart. He said they thought I was a police plant. He told me to go to the local charity shop to get second-hand shorts, T-shirt, a pair of smelly socks and trainers. He told me that, if I wanted to fit in, I had to smell bad like them and be scruffy. He slowly started opening up to me, pointing out individuals, telling me their history. They were ex-murderers, rapists, robbers, drug smugglers and even a pirate.

'I was moved to a small dormitory in the isolation wing, which was kept only for those who were dying or had incurable diseases, I was told. There was one other man in this wing who snored so loudly that he was put into isolation with me, as nobody else could sleep. I never found out why I was put into this place. The following day, the other men befriended me, once they saw I was genuinely distressed and needing help in this environment. The men taught me many things, such as how to rob people and how to check if a prostitute was going to cheat you. I was even given a map to a government gold field, showing where the fence was loose and told how to get inside and which building to go to where equipment and tools were stored to steal. I was also taught how to be aware if somebody was about to attack me and what to do about it. One man asked if I would be a member of his gang when he got out!

'The following day there was a different guard on duty. Most of the others were aloof and overbearing bullies; this man was different. He smiled often and was gentle and respectful to those he interacted with. He had bought a tray of bread (cream buns actually, but I didn't think the kastom men would know what these were) out of his own money as an act of kindness for us, as we were treated with contempt by society as worthless vagrants. This man taught me that, no matter how bad things can get, you can still be compassionate to others. I learned a very valuable lesson.

'The Salvation Army Captain helped me to get a job picking mandarins on a plantation, then paid for my bus fare out of his own money. This was another act of compassion.'

The men fell silent. Chief Nogwaren handed his pipe to the man of a lower grade who had asked the question. The Chiefs and I were called for kava. My brother looked at me and smiled. Nassey offered me my shell, bowing gracefully. After the kava ritual, Donald escorted me back to the restaurant. I was amazed how the jungle changed when darkness fell. I was presented with a plate of dog biscuits and nature identical jam. I was disappointed as I was expecting at least one chicken leg!

By the time I returned to my hut, it was lightly raining. I dozed off and woke at 9.30 pm. I prepared for a stay in the leaf shelter and decided to wait by the restaurant for the Chief, as it would be easier to see him approaching by torchlight. The night sky was full of heavy dark rain clouds which occasionally broke to allow me to see the stars. I watched a firefly chase its tail around my hut on the hill. I heard a couple of crashes and yelps in the restaurant kitchen so guessed that some dogs were in there, licking clean the plates. Then I heard a rustling sound in the jungle behind me. Something was approaching very quickly. Was it Kassoso? I felt excited and somewhat nervous. Suddenly a dog came bursting out of the bushes, shook itself and sneezed, as much as to say, 'Hah. That fooled you.'

It sniffed at my boots then ambled off into the darkness. It began to rain again. I went back to my hut to check my alarm clock. It was 11.30 pm. I laid on my bed fully clothed just in case the Chief was coming later. At least I thought Kassoso would know that I would be either at the nakamal or in my hut, so they knew where to find me. I fell asleep.

Tribal Story   Circumcision   Girl's Cutting Ritual
Sacred Trees

I woke at 1.30 am – no sign of Kassoso. I felt disappointed as another opportunity had been missed. Was this waiting game another subtle test, I wondered. By 5.30 am I could smell wood smoke as the villagers prepared their breakfast, usually the leftovers of the meal the night before. As usual, small children laughed and ran about naked and free. I heard Nahu cleaning up the mess made by the dogs in the kitchen the night before.

Donald arrived whilst I was having breakfast for the question and answer session. Donald said that Kassoso was called Yerama in his native language so I guessed this is where the name Yeramanu came from. Why then had they always referred to the Dragon Men as Kassoso? Donald went on to say that the Christians called Kassoso the devil. He sniggered scornfully, 'Iarueri, Kassoso wear a leaf nambas and are always naked. They are very tall and muscular. The story of Kassoso is only found in Itabu – nowhere else. Everything in the kastom tradition that connects to Kassoso is called Nowdaha. The nakamal at Itabu is for Kassoso through the flying fox spirit stone. The nakamal at Itabu is connected by a road (spirit highway) to another small nakamal up in the mountains by the volcano. You will see many flying foxes there. You know when to hunt flying fox as you see Kassoso spit on the wild kava leaves. If flying fox is hunted before time (out of season) you will find blood, but no body. This is because Kassoso has blocked the hunt. If you continue to hunt after this warning, Kassoso will kill you. As long as you follow the kastom tradition, you are safe. These rituals are for your safety.

'Iarueri, you were taken to this secret nakamal before. We will go again to make the connection. The Chief will wear a rope around his head and right ankle, called a marrow marrow, to connect to the secret nakamal and to make the kastom dance. In the past, Itabu was a small village hidden in the jungle with a few leaf huts that you couldn't see. There is a story, Iarueri, I will tell you.'

Donald shifted his position in the handmade chair to make himself more comfortable. 'A naked man wearing nambas came into the village. Two girls saw him and said, "There is a strange man in our village; we will follow him." The stranger did a kastom dance. He didn't see the two girls watching him from the bushes. As he was leaving he suddenly saw the girls. The girls said to the man that they would follow him. "No," replied the man, "my home is not good for you." The girls followed him even though he warned them to keep away. He came to the Itabu nakamal, where the girls asked him his name. He replied, "My name is Kassoso. Do not follow me. My house is not suitable for you. See my food." Then he broke a stick. He left and went to the secret nakamal where he climbed to the top of a nabanga tree. The two girls sat on the ground waiting for him to come down. Kassoso told the girls to leave but the girls refused and asked him for some food. Kassoso spat down on to the leaves of the wild kava plant. As the girls looked up, they saw him hanging from a branch as a flying fox. He spat again, then went to sleep. The two girls were still waiting at the bottom of the tree. He saw a pig and kava at Green Point nakamal so came down from the tree for the food. The girls followed him to the nakamal. One girl became afraid; the other girl he held tightly then ripped off her arms and legs, rubbing her blood over his body. He then gave her limbs to her family. This had happened several times before with other girls.'

Donald got out of his chair to enact a peculiar walk that Kassoso did, then he laughed. 'It was Kassoso who originally wore nambas which our ancestors copied. Before, we were all naked. When the Christians came, they tried to stop our ways but the old men remembered. The place of origin for Kassoso is called Quatengan. It means the secret for the Chief and his people. Kassoso gave us the kastom teachings, dances and songs. You sleep and Kassoso will give you a song or dance in your dreams. All the people are told the song or dance so they practise and learn it, then perform it in the nakamal for Kassoso. You heard the songs in our native language but in modern days we hear them now in Bislama or English. Everything in our tradition has been given to us from Kassoso.

'Occasionally some songs are given to us from our ancestors. When the Chief wants someone to sing a new song, he will point at you and give you a hoya flower which will help you get the song in your dreams. Before you sleep, you take the hoya flower and go to the grave of your father or mother and ask them to bring you a song when you sleep. The following day you perform it in the nakamal which becomes part of our tribal tradition. Men and women will learn it together. It is very important to get teachings when you sleep. After the Chief has pointed to you to make a new song in the nakamal, you are given priority in the kava ritual and you give thanks to Tamaffa and to the hoya Spirit for what will be brought to you in your sleep. Kassoso only teach men, not women. The women's job is to work and to prepare and cook food for the Chief and the nakamal.'

I pressed Donald to explain why or how circumcision began in kastom culture. I understand that circumcision is done for health or medical concerns, but who initially decided to start this practice and why.

'Kassoso taught circumcision. If a man is not circumcised he is not allowed a wife, then the Chief choses who the boy will marry. The kastom doctor performs the circumcision with a bamboo knife. If a man is not circumcised he is not strong. Pigs and kava are given to the kastom doctor for doing this. When you call to Tamaffa, the boy does not cry. Kassoso tells the Chief that this must be done to the boys. Those boys that go to the Western hospital for circumcision will always cry. A teaching from Kassoso is called nasorian.'

I put more pressure on to Donald to explain more about the origins of circumcision. Donald looked a little uneasy, then looked around him to see that nobody else was listening. 'Iarueri, this is secret. Sometimes Kassoso will cause a circumcision within the womb so the baby is born circumcised naturally. This only happens to babies who will be great chiefs or leaders of some sort. It is a sacred sign. Other males then copied this practice. Majikjiki was born naturally circumcised. The boys to be circumcised are kept away from their mothers until after the ceremony. They have their own separate hut in the nakamal. Only when he eventually sees his mother will the boy cry. Kipson, Peter and the other boys will be circumcised in May next year (2013) after the crops are ready in April for the feast.'

I asked Donald what sort of rite of passage did young girls have in the tribe.

'Girls are cut with a piece of broken glass at the top and bottom of their backs to make the blood flow. The girls are put into a special house where they only wear grass skirts and where the men are not allowed to go. In the afternoon, after the cutting ceremony, the women will sing and take the girls to the river to wash. The girls' wounds are then bathed with coconut milk. When the girls start their moon time, it is a secret ceremony done by the women. When the girl has finished her first period, they have a feast for her. Kassoso taught the women these secrets, even though there are no female Kassoso.'

I found this information fascinating. The Chief arrived, asking if I had dreamt about Kassoso. I hadn't. He smiled at me and said that they told him they were coming at 10 pm tonight to let me touch their staff or power. This is because we called to Tamaffa and prepared the chicken and kava last night at the nakamal. The Chief said he would tell the men that they had to leave the nakamal at 9 pm to allow us both to prepare and to settle in the leaf shelter. I felt so excited!

Donald invited me to go with him into the forest, since he needed to collect a particular kastom medicine plant to help with stomach problems. We left soon afterwards, accompanied by his two dogs Kimo and Mickey. I remembered

Donald asking me on our last visit to Itabu if I had had a dog. I told him that I didn't, but as a boy I did and he was called Mickey. Donald said he had remembered the name and called his dog Mickey to honour my dog. Both of Donald's dogs were a light tan colour with large powerful heads. They looked as if their ancestors were dingoes. I remembered that Australian and Hungarian scientists had found that the dingo and wolf still maintain a high degree of intelligence, but domestically bred dogs, especially pedigrees have had their intelligence bred out to improve their looks, ie looks bred in, intelligence bred out as their brains become smaller. There are a few exceptions, such as the Welsh sheepdog. One could say that the same applies to the noble families of Europe!

We walked along the jungle trails, the dappled sunlight sparkling on droplets of the early morning rain hanging from foliage. I loved the smell of the damp earth and tropical decay underfoot. The forest was alive with secret sounds, yet it was silent to those who could not hear. We passed a large tree in the forest at the edge of the village boundary which had a hollow centre, but open to one side. Donald explained that this tree was used as a tam tam drum for calling the tribe together (skin drums cannot be used in hot humid environments, as the skins cannot be kept taut and rot quickly). The tribe uses hollowed out logs, known as slit drums or trees such as this, to beat with clubs. The hollow centre creates an echo-like sound that travels long distances through the forest.

All around us were giant nabanga trees where aerial roots reached to the ground like pillars supporting ancient temples. At times it was surprisingly dark where the tree canopies were the thickest, little light reaching the forest floor. These places were the secret domain of fungi that glowed with a luminescent blue light (the only other place I have seen luminescent algae is in the sacred places of Cornwall). The nabanga tree is central to the spiritual culture and power of the kastom people in this land. It is where the Chiefs gain their authority and power by talking to the ancient and wise nabanga spirits.

There used to be a similar situation in the West prior to the targeted destruction of the ancient master trees and sacred groves of Europe by the invading Roman Empire, followed by Christianity, who wanted to disempower our Pagan and Heathen ancestors. The kastom people throughout the world understand about working with the spirits of the trees, especially the ancient master trees which are the wisdom keepers of tribal culture. When performing ceremony, you always ask for permission to enter into the sacred personal space of the tree; in other words, trees which hold occult magical power that they permit us to work with.

It is very important that the reader understands the true meaning of the words occult, Pagan and Heathen. Occult simply means "that which is unseen". Even today in the medical profession, if a doctor cannot locate the point of origin of internal bleeding, it is officially known as an occult bleed. In kastom usage, it means the spirit world. Pagan simply means "a dweller in the country", ie the wild places. Heathen simply means "a dweller on the heath", ie the mountains. When the Christian missionaries came to subdue our ancestors, they usually came by ship or boat, so the coastal and river communities were the first to be dominated. It was more difficult to make their way inland to reach the Pagans and very difficult to get into the mountains to the Heathens. As usual the Church has twisted the origins of these ancient meanings.

When two sacred or master trees are growing next to each other, a natural energetic portal is created and activated – a place of interaction between the worlds. It is from such energetic interfaces that the Kassoso come and go. This is an especially powerful phenomenon if these trees are growing over fire (Fire Dragon energy), such as the volcano at Itabu, or water (Water Dragon energy) in the Celtic lands. Scientists have the technology now to measure these energy fields resonating between trees and have called it the "biofield" (this is a fancy word for the aura).

We came to a clearing in the forest where coconut trees had been planted long ago. Donald opened a couple with his teeth and machete for us to eat. The dogs principally ate coconut flesh; meat was a luxury for them. As we ate, Donald retold me the story of the tribal creation myth.

We re-entered the thick jungle where Donald found the herb he was looking for. It was a plant that looked like it belonged to the nettle family. He took several cuttings which he said he would plant in his garden at home. Donald showed me a nabanga tree nearby which was hollow and within this space were hundreds of small bats roosting. Donald threw a stick into the roost which caused many to fly and wheel around our heads. Donald said that the bats were good to eat. He explained how you climbed up inside the tree to pick the young bats from their roost before they were strong enough to fly away.

As we continued along a disused track, Donald stopped me and showed me a thin vine that was stretching across the path at various heights. He showed me the vine closely; it had small saw-like "teeth" along it. Donald said that, if you ran into one of these when you were chasing a pig, it could cut your throat wide open and kill you or trip you up, cutting you to the bone. He cut it down with his machete.

Donald then took me to see a nawaias tree which featured strongly in the tribal creation myth. It was the most amazing tree I have ever seen. The large tree had grown normally but at its base it had formed what I can only describe as a wooden font, a structure that was living and full of water. Initially I thought that someone had trained the tree to grow this way but Donald assured me that it was a perfectly natural phenomenon.

As we made our way back to Itabu, I was shown wild peanuts and wild passion fruit amongst other tropical species I didn't recognise. On our arrival back at the village I was given a fresh coconut to drink its "milk" and given another fried greasy cold egg for lunch. The women had been into my hut to change my sheets. I was given a pink satin sheet this time! The weather was sticky, hot and humid, with occasional light showers. Jack and his wife returned from hospital with Frankie; the baby was fine now. The doctor said he had a back problem (which is where the magic stone indicated there was an energy block) and was given several injections.

By 3 pm it had turned cloudy and cold. Unfortunately, heavy rain looked imminent. I tried to connect with Kassoso but I couldn't settle; I was too cold. As I stood outside of my hut waiting for the call to go to the nakamal, I saw an eagle circling directly above me then it flew off towards the volcano. I thought that this was a good omen.

I was called to go to the nakamal just after 5 pm. There were only four boys present, plus Donald and me. The Chief, I was told, was in Sergay village taking kava. Donald cut up a dead branch with his machete, sending a small boy off to the village to bring back a smouldering piece of wood from their fire to start a fire in the nakamal. Donald gathered dried palm fronds together, placing the glowing stick in the centre, and blew upon it to bring the flames roaring back to life. One of the older youths was called Chone. He seemed to be at the nakamal most nights; he always wore a ragged yellow vest.

After the kava ritual I returned to the restaurant for my meal, which was more dog biscuits and an unripe tomato. As the Ceylon tea from Fiji had finished, it was replaced with a small jar of instant coffee, also a product of Fiji.

I returned to my hut to wait for the Chief to call for me to go to the nakamal to meet Kassoso. By 9.30 pm there was still no sign of him. I began to pace up and down, feeling anxious, as Kassoso had told the Chief they would connect with me at 10 pm. Was the Chief asleep, sick, drunk with kava; had he been called out to another village drama or had just decided not to turn up?

By the time 9.45 pm had come I decided I wasn't going to wait any longer so set off on my own along the trail to the nakamal by torchlight. Maybe the Chief was waiting for me at Donald's encampment. I reached the boundary of Donald's little settlement and waited. I shone my torch on to the huts purposefully to let people know I was there – no response. I called softly, but loud enough for anyone awake to hear me, as expected in tribal kastom protocol – still no response.

By now it was almost 10 pm. I passed silently between the leaf huts and on to the nakamal, crawling into the leaf shelter. Luminescent fungi growing at the edge of the nakamal lit the undergrowth like blue LED lights. The leaf shelter was empty of all mats, bedding and mosquito net. Everything had been removed, probably to stop them getting wet in the rain, but should have been in the shelter for tonight. I lay on the bare earth amongst the leaves and twigs, settling down as best I could, praying to Kassoso that I was in the shelter and waiting for their visit. The mosquito scout sent word out that there was a free buffet available; within minutes whining mosquitoes were attacking my face, hands and ankles. I tucked my trousers into my socks and pulled down the sleeves of my sweatshirt to cover my hands. An insect crawled into my shirt, which I managed to get out. I laid my lower ear on to my arm as a pillow to prevent insects crawling into it. I waited. I could smell the last curls of woodsmoke drifting on the breeze from the dying nakamal fire and the sweet perfume of the hoya blossoms. The night sky was heavy with rain clouds, which occasionally separated to let me see the stars. Yasur volcano exploded occasionally and I heard the flying foxes foraging through the trees.

I knew I had to try to sleep, for it was in this state only that Kassoso came in their physical form. I dozed off then heard something unusual. I was aware of and used to the sounds of the flying fox flying amongst the trees; it was a familiar sound, yet there was something different happening. Suddenly, I was awake and alert as I heard the approaching wing beats of a very large creature which I estimated to be the size of a large swan, or bigger. Whatever this being was, it landed heavily on the ground near to where the shelter was then I heard footsteps coming towards me. Was this Kassoso or even an angel? I held my breath as I searched for a form or figure in the darkness that I could relate to. I could see nothing at all, yet I could hear this creature walking slowly around the shelter. I knew it was staring at me. I could feel its gaze.

I focused my intent and will to look shamanically through the gaps in the palm fronds and saw the large black stooped figure of a creature half man and half flying fox. As soon as it realised it had been seen, it disappeared into the blackness of the forest. This had to be Kassoso, an interdimensional materialisation known technically, I suppose, as a were-bat.

When something like this happens, it challenges your rational mind; you have to look at the bigger picture.

19th October 2012:
Spirit Sickness   Chief's Cell Phone

I sensed it was about 2 am. Kassoso didn't come physically to offer me their staff of power. Shortly afterwards, it began to rain. When the rain became heavy and started pouring through the leaf shelter, soaking me, I decided to return to my hut. As I passed through Donald's encampment a dog, sheltering under a hut, raised its head to stare at me. Thankfully it didn't bark.

I looked at my alarm clock when I arrived at my hut; it was 3 am. I slipped into bed, pulling burrs out of my hair and beard. It poured down for the rest of the night. I woke at 6 am. There was no obvious sign of Kassoso. I felt disappointed and somewhat frustrated.

I went for breakfast at 7 am as usual, where I found Donald waiting for me. I told Donald that I had spent the night at the nakamal. He said the Chief had spoken to him at dawn to say he had had a dream and that we are to connect with Kassoso again tonight at the nakamal. Breakfast was instant coffee and dog biscuits – no Pakistan jam in sight.

I did my last laundry before leaving Itabu, as I had to allow two full days for the clothes to dry, should it remain wet. Melissa called for me for lunch at 10.30 am. The Chief had assigned her to help Nahu in the kitchen. Today I had a warm greasy egg with cucumber.

I returned to my hut to pray to Kassoso and to connect as best I could. I did a shamanic journey, connecting with the Dragon of Crystal and Fire, which I saw emerging from the depths of the volcano crater. Once free, it stretched out its flaming wings and took to the air.

By 3 pm more rain clouds had gathered, causing the temperature to drop considerably. The Chief called for me at 5 pm to go to the nakamal. He apologised for not coming last night but gave no reason. I asked for none. What is done is done. Kenneth from Erromango was at the nakamal. The Chief asked me if I recognised him, which I did, offering my hand to shake his. He was pleased I remembered his name. The sacred fire was already lit and several men gathered around it. Kenneth asked me to describe to the other men how I opened skulls in the hospital mortuary. It obviously had reactivated some deep cellular memory of past times. After relating the techniques along with hand movements and dramatic sounds to enhance the story, I felt suddenly ill. I felt feverishly hot, then began to sweat profusely and had severe abdominal cramps with the sensation of urgently needing the toilet. I hung on until the end of the kava ritual, where miraculously the sickness left me completely. Maggie refers to these experiences as "spirit sickness" where an energetic adjustment had taken place.

Dinner was bread and cucumber. Somebody had obviously been to the market during the day. Donald told me to wait for the Chief who would come for me later to go to the nakamal to meet Kassoso. I connected with them as best I could.

At 8.30 pm the Chief arrived. We walked in silence to the nakamal. When we arrived at our leaf shelter it was all prepared as before – mosquito nets, along with mats and bedding. We rolled up the net, securing it over the cross pole of the shelter. The mosquitoes had a choice of menu now. We settled down to sleep. The mosquitoes were savage and came in legions. The Chief shouted, 'Mosquito,' covering his head with his sheet. It wasn't long before the Chief went into human zoo mode again, coughing, sneezing, farting and moaning. At one point he made a good impression of a horse neighing!

I stared into the darkness, following the flight paths of passing fireflies as they moved through the nakamal. Again the Chief had assured me that Kassoso would come at 10 pm. I sensed it was almost midnight and there was still no sign of Kassoso. The Chief's cell phone went off! I was furious. Each night I had made a point of checking with him that his mobile phone was off or at least on silent. 'Yes,' was the reply each time. Why would you want to bring a mobile phone with you on an important occasion such as this anyway, especially when the Chief had stressed to me that Kassoso did not like modern technology?

Mobile phones are my pet "hate". They are a curse of modern Western society that destroys sacred silence and creates sickness from harmful emissions. When I first came to Itabu in 2003, there were no cell phones. Now because of advertising through fear-based propaganda, everyone wants a mobile phone, so the Telecom companies offered "buy one, get one free" at very low costs. Of course, once the local people were hooked, they would then have to buy expensive top up credits. The greedy corporations had tapped into vulnerable captive consumers. (More Asians have access to a mobile phone than a toilet!

When health and sanitation of people come second to cell phones, it is a disgrace. – APEC Seminar, Russia, 2012.)

The Chief scrambled in the darkness to find his phone. He put it on, which caused the phone to light the shelter up like a searchlight. He apologised. I thought cannibalism should be reinstated. We settled down again. The pillows had come from Donald's encampment where all of the children were crawling with head lice. I hoped I wouldn't get a dose. When I lived with the Attié tribe in the Ivory Coast, the mothers bought and crushed mothballs, rubbing the naphthalene into the heads of their children to kill the lice. It began to rain.

Part 3
The Knowing

20th October 2012
Secret Nakamal   Kassoso Hand

We both crawled out of the leaf shelter to urinate. The Chief's cell phone went off again! I could have hit the man on the back of the skull. The rain became heavier. The Chief decided to call off the vigil and return to his hut to sleep. The Chief said, 'My brother, Kassoso should have come. Something is wrong. We will have to talk about it tomorrow.'

We left the nakamal and I left him at Donald's village, returning to my hut on the hill. I looked at my alarm clock; it was 1.30 am. I felt very annoyed and disappointed. I had one more night left at Itabu to make the sacred physical connection.

I woke at 5.15 am to the sound of rain on the thatch and a distant tam tam slit drum being played across the valley somewhere. Nahu was already raking up fallen leaves around the restaurant area. A baby cried then children started to laugh on waking.

It was my last full day at Itabu with my tribal family. I felt sad, especially since I had already decided that this would be my final visit to the tribe. I had completed all of my initiations and ceremonies except receiving the "power" from the Kassoso stick. If no connection was made tonight, then maybe Kassoso would connect with me on Manannan's Island once I had created my own nakamal and made the spirit highway back to Itabu.

At 6.30 am I heard the Chief having a heated discussion with someone. It sounded as if he was reprimanding one of his family for some reason. Breakfast was bread with nature identical flavoured raspberry jam and instant coffee. It appeared that the jam thieves had emptied the mango jar. I had to go to the toilet quickly, as I had diarrhoea. A large brown spider crawled out of the hole of the toilet box just before I sat down. We exchanged greetings.

The Chief arrived at the restaurant at 7.15 am. He was really upset that Kassoso had not come at 10 pm as they told him they would do on two occasions in different dreams.

'Iarueri, after we left the nakamal early this morning, I spoke to Kassoso and asked them why they had lied to me. I told them that my heart is sad because Iarueri needs to touch your stick and he has no more time left.'

I felt sorry for my brother. He was clearly distressed as this had never happened to him before. He had lost face but also confidence in his connection with Spirit. He spoke again, 'Kassoso said to me that they were no longer happy in coming to the nakamal, so we will try another way, my brother. I have killed two pigs and a chicken. Kassoso know this. I will call Donald and you and he will go up to the secret nakamal at the volcano, not on the tourist path but the path that Kassoso use (the dangerous one). At the top, Donald will give you a stone and mynesi leaves. When you come to the nakamal tonight for the last time, we will call Kassoso again at kava time to show him we have opened a new road for them to travel along. I am very upset that Kassoso have lied to me.'

The Chief's beliefs had been challenged with this situation so it was vital that the new plan was successful for both of our sakes. The Chief asked for some more money to buy kava for tonight. He repeated what he had said several times before and that was, even though he had money, Kassoso needed to know that I had provided the kava for them.

The Chief spoke again, 'Iarueri, the harder you try to connect to Kassoso, the stronger the power given to you when they decide to link. We will wait for the rain to go off and for the jungle to dry a little before Donald takes you to the secret nakamal, otherwise you will get very wet and the steep path will be slippery and dangerous.'

I realised that the Chief and Donald were doing everything that they could possibly do to help me link with Kassoso. I think this is a testing time for all of us at the moment. Before the Chief left, he added, 'Donald is my firstborn son. I have taught him the secrets, so when I die he will be the next High Chief.'

I asked the Chief to book a truck for me for 9.30 am tomorrow to take me to the airport. The Chief said he would arrange it. He looked sad and tearful.

As I waited for Donald to come to my hut, I prayed to Kassoso to give me their secrets to allow me to receive their blessings and wisdom through touching their sacred stick. Donald arrived earlier than expected and said that the rain and wind were going to get stronger, so we must leave straight away.

We left the village at 8.30 am, passing through Donald's settlement and saw Donald's son, Wai Wai, wearing a split football over his head like a motorcycle helmet. He looked so funny. Another small boy dragged a large aluminium bowl across the ground, which contained a baby. Namu was looking after two wild piglets that Kimo had separated from their mother. One was tethered by a back leg, the other Namu held in her lap. They will be reared as domesticated pigs. I wondered if the nursing mothers in this country suckled piglets at their breast, as the women do in Papua New Guinea. I decided it was inappropriate to ask.

We arrived at the Itabu nakamal, where Chone was waiting for us. Donald picked some mynesi growing on his grandfather's grave for us. We set off, accompanied by three of Donald's dogs, Kimo, Mickey and Chika. Soon after starting our ascent of the steep jungle trail, the dogs spotted a wild rooster, gave it chase, but he got away by flying up into a high tree. Chone tried throwing stones at it but couldn't get a clear shot because of the branches. When we reached a certain place, about three-quarters of the way up, Donald picked out two palm-sized round volcanic stones – one was for me to hold for flying fox, the other for him for Yasur. The path was arduous, slippery and very dangerous. Erosion had eaten away at the most precipitous sections of the path, which fell away into deep ravines. The dogs were a nuisance as they kept barging past us, causing us to trip, or kept getting under our feet.

We had a break. Chone climbed up a twisted coconut tree which overhung a steep slope. He cut down large round green coconuts, throwing some of them down to Donald and me; the rest dropped on to the ground and rolled down the hill; some escaped, crashing into the undergrowth far below; one hit Kimo. Donald and I managed to catch a few as they rolled towards us. Donald cut open a couple of coconuts, showing me the three "eyes" at the end. He explained that this was the secret face of Kassoso. We drank the refreshing milk and pressed on.

We arrived at the secret nakamal at the top of Mt Kerroukneri. This was the first time Chone had been here so he was very excited. Since my last visit a Kassoso stone had been positioned in the west of the nakamal and the gardens surrounding it were still maintained by someone. The leaf hut was still not completed. It was very windy and exposed and we were directly opposite Yasur crater across the stone flats leading from the track the tourists used far below us. I was perspiring after the climb and felt chilly now. Donald and Chone were excited as they found two coconut shells, a bark sieve, a stirring stick and some old kava roots near to the place where the sacred fire had been lit. Donald said that this was good as we could drink kava on the Kassoso path here at their secret nakamal opposite Yasur volcano.

Chone prepared the kava as Donald disappeared into the rain forest with the mynesi and stones to place them in a secret place where he could talk to Kassoso to ask them to come tonight to talk to me. I was not permitted to go with Donald so watched Chone prepare the kava in the traditional manner when there is only one person to do it. It was quite an art. Two split sticks were knocked into the ground with a stone as anchoring points for the bark sieve to be secured to. As we had no water, coconut milk was used to mix with the masticated kava root. The juice dribbled from the sieve as it was wrung out like a wet towel, then stirred with the stick into the coconut shells. Donald returned to help with the process. He said that Chone and I had to drink together as this was Chone's first visit to the secret nakamal. The kava was very strong and bitter. I could only drink a little so Chone finished my shell. We asked Kassoso to come to Itabu tonight, thanking them for coming down the new road.

It began to rain horizontally; I felt very cold. Yasur poured out thick white smoke from his crater into the black rain clouds. His explosions were impressive. I respected Yasur. I asked Donald why he never wore an ear stick. He replied that he would do so when he became High Chief. I had decided not to continue to wear my ear stick any longer if Kassoso did not give me proof of physical connection. We chatted for a while together. Donald told me another story about two men fighting, so it ended up with Donald and Chone removing their shirts to enact the fight for me. The wind and rain became stronger so we decided to return to Itabu.

As we descended down the steep slope, the heavens opened and we found ourselves in a tropical downpour on a very dangerous path; I slipped often. We decided to shelter beneath some tree ferns, but the rain didn't ease, so Donald said that we must press on regardless. We were soaked to the skin, cold and miserable. Donald said he didn't like the cold rain. I tripped over a root across the steep path and fell, sliding in the mud; my clothing was filthy. Donald and Chone were concerned and came running to my aid but soon laughed when they realised I was unhurt.

When we had reached the end of the steep descending path we were able to walk with ease through the rain forest. The local men had no difficulty hiking up and down steep slopes but complained of sore legs when we walked long distances on the flat. The dogs flushed out a wild chicken from the undergrowth which flew off into the trees, making a loud noise. Sadly she left behind one of her small black chicks which went to ground between the root crevices of a fern. Chone dug it out with a stick and put it into his pocket to rear it at his house. Not far away the dogs found four eggs but they appeared to be abandoned, as they were cold. Chone decided to take them anyway.

Donald wanted to collect two stones for me to take for my nakamal at home on Manannan's Island. He searched amongst stones in an old riverbed, still not yet active from the rains, until he found what he wanted – two stones, one black to represent the boar and the other red to represent Yasur volcano. They were palm-sized and smooth. Donald said these stones were a gift from Kassoso; they had heard our prayers.

By the time we had reached Itabu it was after 1 pm. I felt like a mole which had just emerged from a hole in the ground. After changing my wet clothes, I was called for lunch which was two cold greasy eggs mangled into a heap on my plate. I struggled to get them down. What I really needed was a hot cup of tea but none came.

After lunch I washed my muddy clothes, hoping that they would be dry enough for my early departure tomorrow. I spent the remaining time in the afternoon praying to Kassoso to come tonight, my last night, and that the rain would stop to enable the Chief and I to sleep in the nakamal if that was his decision.

At 5 pm Donald came to escort me to the nakamal for our last kava ritual together. Thankfully the rain had stopped, revealing a clear starlit sky with a beautiful crescent moon. I took my place by the sacred fire, glad of its light and warmth, enjoying the smell of the woodsmoke which always seemed to bring a sense of inner peace to me. I listened to the sounds of the rain forest, taking in the sights, sounds and smells for the last time. I felt sad that I would not return to Itabu again but I knew that I could always connect with the Chief at the nakamal through my shamanic journeys, probably at a deeper spiritual level.

The Chief arrived, followed by another man who carried the kava roots. The Chief took the kava from the man and placed the roots in the centre of the nakamal, then called to me to come and pick them up to give to him, which I did. This was to show Kassoso I had provided the kava for them to drink. After the kava ritual, I said my goodbyes to the men gathered. I was escorted back to my hut by the Chief who asked me to wait until called for my meal as he had arranged a gathering that would be shared by others as a "feast" to honour me. He told me that we had to leave at 7 am in the morning because of the continuous delays with the construction traffic building the new highway. He disappeared into the night.

I was called for dinner at 7 pm. Several men were present to share the meal of rice, noodles and tinned fish. The Chief gave a speech thanking me for coming to Itabu and I responded to all gathered thanking them for including me as a member of their family. They all clapped and laughed. The Chief and the other men piled their plates high with food and left to return to the nakamal to drink more kava. Donald stayed behind with me. As the Chief left, he whispered to me to be ready for when he came later to go to meet Kassoso at the nakamal. Donald escorted me back to my hut after my meal then left to join the others. This was the first time that the Chief and I had not worn nambas. Another indication of tradition dying out.

The Chief arrived at my hut at 10 pm. He was drunk with kava, swaying, unsteady on his feet and his speech was slurred. He almost fell so I grabbed him by the arm to support him. The Chief said to me that Kassoso said that it was going to rain tonight so I was to stay in my leaf hut and they would come to me here. I didn't know whether to be annoyed with the Chief or pleased about the message from Kassoso. The Chief always got drunk on our last night together, so part of me expected this to happen, but secretly I was hoping that tonight, my last night with the tribe, he would have been alert and focussed for this sacred magical encounter together. I had to trust Spirit now and let go of all expectations. I thanked the Chief as he stumbled off into the darkness, belching loudly.

I went to bed to try to sleep. I must have dozed off, surrendering to the universe, as I was woken by a light tapping sound at the window next to my bed. I shone my small torch quickly at my alarm clock; it was just after 11 pm. The tapping resumed. Was it Kassoso? I reached up into the darkness to the open window and felt a hand gently grasp mine. For some reason, it felt as though the hand had a bandage wrapped around it or wore some sort of glove. It wasn't bare skin. There was no staff or stick offered either. Then the hand gently squeezed mine and slowly pulled away, our fingertips touching before it disappeared into the blackness of the night. I sat upright in my bed, eyes wide open, praying that Kassoso would return. They never did.

I felt ecstatic that some sort of physical contact had been made again, but I also felt that there was something that was still incomplete after the nine years of this preparation and training. There was no sense of "power" being given to me, nor was there any clear proof of authenticity. Doubts started flooding into my mind; was it really the hand of Kassoso or was it one of the men playing a cruel game? I didn't know and, because of this lack of proof beyond doubt, I felt bereft, almost empty, after all that I had been through over the years, now to fail, as I saw it, at the final hurdle. I knew that there was still a chance that Kassoso would come to Manannan's Island so I needed to create my own nakamal at home on my return which would involve a lot of hard work in our garden to prepare and to create that sacred space. I realised for Kassoso to come, this difficult task had to be done. I knew that if I did nothing then nothing would happen. If I did something then something may happen. If I kept on doing what I was doing then I would keep on getting what I was getting. Therefore, I had to change something within me and also within my home environment to enable Kassoso and I to create, as the Chief would say, "a new road" for us to make the appropriate connection. I hoped that these last few days of disappointment would not affect the Chief's connection to Kassoso either.

I couldn't sleep, as my mind was too active, so I tried as best as I could to rest and I eventually dozed off.

Chief's carving   National Elections   Return to Vila

I woke at 5 am. I went to the restaurant for breakfast at 6 am. The Chief arrived soon afterwards, telling me that he had had a dream where his father had come to him and was very pleased that I had gone up to the mountain to the secret nakamal. He also said that he had spoken to Kassoso but didn't tell me what they had said. I told the Chief about my experience with the hand last night. He smiled broadly and said that that was very good, as Kassoso would bring information to me in my dreams now and help me in my life. I told the Chief that I felt no "power" (energy). He replied that that didn't matter but what was important was that Kassoso had held my hand after ceremony.

I asked the Chief again for permission to tell the people in the West about the Kassoso story. He said, 'No. This is a secret story for you only, Iarueri.'

I felt very disappointed with this statement but agreed to keep the story secret. The Chief thanked me for coming and asked when Natu and I would return to Itabu. I replied that, if we were to return, it would take us two years to save enough money for the expensive air fares and travel costs. I didn't have the heart to tell him that I had already decided that I would not be coming back and I would never see my brother again.

The Chief asked me to take photos of our house and village in Manannan's Island to send to him, reminding me of how important it was for me to do the ceremony with the fish in my nakamal at home. He said he wanted a photo of me cooking the fish over my nakamal fire as proof! I agreed.

The truck arrived at 7 am. We hoped there would be no unexpected travel delays. Donald came to say goodbye. He gave me two small stone carvings that he had made. Namu, Nahu, Melissa and Frankie's mother, plus a lady I had given healing to but didn't know her name, gave me boar's tusk necklaces as gifts for Natu. The Chief came to me when the others had left and secretively gave me a small figure of a man's face which he had made himself to help me connect with Kassoso. The figure was very basic and simple, made from red volcanic clay, moulded by hand into a short sausage shape with crude facial markings scratched into it. This was the first time in nine years that the Chief had given me a gift of this nature.

We left Itabu for Lenakel at 8 am. Most of the village had gathered to see me off. When it was time to leave the Chief's family and others piled into the back of the truck, including Enoch. As we approached the volcanic ash plain, we met two other trucks converging with us simultaneously from two other side roads. All three truck drivers decided to have a race to see who could get to the river crossing first. It was a reckless activity which covered everybody in black ash and almost ended in one of the vehicles turning over. Our driver backed off at the last minute to let another driver pass as we descended to the fast-flowing river. The race continued on the other side of the river until we reached the principal road not far from where the Chief had had his accident. The Chief looked nervous the entire time and it was he who told the driver to back off. He held his broken hand close to his chest to support it as the truck jumped and crashed over the ruts.

Enoch was dropped off at the village he now lived in. It was election time at the end of the month in Vanuatu so for the last few days trucks had been driving up and down the main road past Itabu with loudspeakers blaring party songs with banners and flags to encourage the local people to vote. The nearer we approached Lenakel, the more banners, flags and posters we saw. The local people I spoke to said it was all a show; none trusted any of the politicians as they said that they were all corrupt. What's new?

We had been expecting long hold-ups with the construction traffic and work gangs building the new highway but were not delayed at all, arriving at Lenakel much earlier than expected. We dropped the others off at the market to shop and then parked the truck near to the sea to talk. We saw a taxi bus drive over a steep bank, ripping off the rear bumper bar. He stopped, reversed, picked up the bumper and threw it through an open window on to the back seat, then drove off. We all laughed.

I have seen several minor traffic accidents in Vanuatu, but nothing like the terrible road accidents I have witnessed in India. On one occasion I was returning from an ashram to Bangalore in a taxi with a friend where we had to manoeuvre off the highway because of a shocking accident. A cement truck had run over a motorcycle which was carrying eight members of the same family (yes, eight!). Everyone who was on the bike was lying in the road dead. Everybody had horrendous injuries, including the mother who had had the top of her skull severed cleanly off, revealing an empty cranium. There was no brain and, surprisingly, no blood. Onlookers stood and stared but nobody did anything. I suppose because there wasn't anything that anybody could do.

On another occasion a few years later I was returning from the same ashram. I witnessed a hit and run accident where a man was knocked off his motorcycle and run over. His legs were smashed. I stopped my taxi and we lifted him into the vehicle, blood pouring everywhere. He was screaming. The taxi driver was not happy. We took the man to the nearest hospital as quickly as we could and I gave the taxi driver extra money to clean up the mess. Everywhere I went in India I saw abandoned smashed cars and trucks at the side of the roads. Thankfully, it wasn't that bad in Vanuatu.

On the way to the airport the driver of our truck decided to overtake a slower vehicle and, in so doing, drove straight into a hen with her chicks, which were slowly crossing the road. The hen and chicks were scattered in all directions. I felt sick.

We arrived at the airport in good time so I checked in. The driver parked the truck in the shade and went to sleep. The Chief and Jack waited with me for my call to board. Jack wandered off to speak to one of his friends so the Chief held me gently by the arm and spoke.

'Iarueri, hold the red stone (carving) in your right hand with the fresh fish when you do the ceremony in your nakamal on Manannan's Island, calling to Majikjiki and Kassoso.'

It was time to go. I embraced my brother. He looked at his feet for I knew that, if his eyes had met mine, he would have cried. I shook Jack's hand and went through to departures, boarding the small aircraft immediately. It was a 17-seater which had torn dirty seats and some of the interior fittings were hanging off, especially around the windows. Most of the internal signs in the plane were in Chinese. The plane had left half an hour early, as all passengers were on board. The ride was turbulent and noisy but we landed at Port Vila in one piece.

I got a taxi to Liz's house. Liz had told me where the door key was hidden so I let myself in and had a shower. It was so pleasant to have a proper wash. Liz arrived home from work and we went to Ronnie's nakamal so that Liz and her friends could drink kava and catch up on their local news. On our return back home, Liz made a homemade stew for dinner which was delicious – my first decent meal for many days. I was tired so went to bed early, with the Chief's carving under my pillow, calling to Kassoso. The bed was so comfortable. One of the main lessons I had learned from the Chief was "respect".

22nd October 2012:
Travel Home
I slept well for the first time in days. I was up at 5 am to prepare for my departure. I walked into town to get a cooked breakfast, followed by chocolate! It began to rain. I wanted to buy Maggie a present so changed some traveller's cheques to buy her a

boar's tusk choker on a silver chain. Liz had kindly organised for Joel to take me to the airport. She had been a wonderful help and support.

I boarded my flight to Brisbane then changed flights on to Singapore, where I spent another couple of days praying to Kassoso and writing up my pocket book notes into my journal. I removed my ear stick.

After leaving Singapore and a change of flight in Dubai, then an overnight stay near Gatwick Airport in London, I eventually arrived home to the Isle of Man on 26th October. Maggie was at the airport to meet me. I fell into her loving arms.

During my journey home from Vanuatu, I pondered constantly about the dilemma I faced with the Chief not giving me permission to tell this part of his story this time. After I had been home and settled for a few days, I wrote a letter to my brother, asking for permission again, expecting his reply within six weeks. None came. Life got in the way, as it does, so I never got around to creating my personal nakamal in the garden, as I said I would. I knew that I needed the Chief's permission to galvanise me into action. Even though the Chief and I were no longer together physically, I knew I could still connect with him, Kassoso and the Dragon Riders through my shamanic dreaming. I journeyed often to the nakamal at Itabu to connect with my brother, sometimes just to sit in silence with him by the sacred fire or to receive one of his teachings. I did some energy work at "Dragon's Gate" on the Isle of Man to help ground and facilitate the movement of the Dragon Riders from their different dimensions, accessing the island as one of their bases in third dimension.

26th December 2012:
Kassoso staff

In a shamanic journey, along with my spirit allies, I made a strong connection to Kassoso at last. What a joyful reunion! I journeyed to the nakamal at Itabu where I saw three Kassoso standing at the portal of the spirit highway leading from the volcano. I went to them and one, who I guessed was the leader, offered to me his sacred stick which I grasped gently. I was pulled through the portal, finding myself inside Yasur volcano. The three Kassoso were silhouetted black against the intensely bright realm of fire. Kassoso indicated for me to follow them as they guided me into the inferno.

At first I felt a little afraid but also felt confident that all was well. I maintained my hold of the Kassoso stick, this being the only form of "reality" I had in the maelstrom of molten rock, heat, flames and intense noise. It sounded as though I was in the centre of ten thousand crematorium furnaces. At some point, I cannot exactly tell when, I felt my body being incinerated into ash within seconds, yet my soul, or whatever aspect of me it was, began to ascend through a column of fire which burnt away old belief systems, programming, indoctrination and finally the illusion of my ego. Eventually I became one with the Dragon of the Molten Seas, feeling a great inner peace of what I can only describe as the "I am presence". I then rose upwards into the sun.

At that point, the great cosmic dragons arrived with their riders. Tangarua was one of the leaders. I was invited to take my place as a Dragon Rider and a Kassoso staff was given to me. Tangarua activated the sacred stick, causing a pulse of crystalline purple light that filled the space around me. I felt liquid, fluid, flame-like. I knew, had I decided to do so, I could have shapeshifted into any form I chose. Then I noticed a speck of light far below me. It was my home planet – Earth. We descended and I regained my human form as a being of crystal and fire, passing back through the portal to the Itabu nakamal.

17th January 2013:
Permission given

I had still not received a reply from the Chief regarding permission to publish so a couple of days ago I e-mailed Liz in Port Vila and asked her to get Joel to contact the Chief or Michael, who should be back from New Caledonia now, to put my request to the Chief in Bislama so he would understand more clearly. I asked that no coercion or persuasion was to be used because it was very important that the Chief gave his permission freely and with clarity of mind. I explained that, if the Chief and Donald were both killed in a road accident, then the tribal secrets would be lost forever, except for the small amounts that I knew. I also knew that the Chief would kill a pig and drink kava to offer to Kassoso to ask them what they wanted to be done so, in essence, Kassoso were making this decision.

I received an e-mail back from Liz today copying in a letter written in Bislama by Michael which gave me permission from the Chief to tell the story. Liz had translated it into English for me. I was free to publish this amazing story at last. I began work in the garden immediately, cutting down hedges and clearing a space at the bottom of our garden to create our own nakamal, as Maggie can also use it for her sacred female mysteries ceremonies (this task would take many months and during that time we had the worse snowfall for 50 years which held everything up).

Some weeks ago I had done a shamanic journey to meet the Chief at the nakamal at Itabu, asking him for permission to publish his story. He had clearly said yes, but I didn't trust the information I had received, since I didn't really know if it was wishful thinking on my part. I needed an outside intervention to take place because

I didn't want to publish tribal secrets without permission. This would be breaking kastom law and there would be consequences to face.

Now I had permission, I needed to reconnect with my brother shamanically to thank him and to receive his counsel. I went into a space of shamanic dreaming, journeying to the nakamal at Itabu. I found the Chief sitting at the sacred fire, along with Donald and Nikwei at the base of the nabanga tree. The kava ritual had been completed, the other men had left. Part of me yearned to be with them physically again but I knew that connecting with my brother in this way was a way of finding his truth. Nikwei stood and laughed, embracing me, calling me some derogatory name and I him. This was the usual way we greeted each other! Both the Chief and Donald smiled, stood and embraced me. I needed a moment to sit in the silence of the night at the fire with my soul friends, my brothers, to help me to become fully present and grounded at that level of consciousness.

I paid attention to the small details around me – the crackling fire, the smoke stinging my eyes, the sound of the cicadas and flying fox. I drew in the aroma of the woodsmoke and the damp tropical earth. I saw the red glow of Yasur volcano in the darkness nearby and the shining disc of the full moon which cast eerie shadows across the nakamal.

The Chief placed a piece of roasted pig flesh on a leaf plate beside me on the log on which I sat, my fingers tracing the knotted log and its burnt end. I felt deeply at peace, grounded and present in that moment. When I was ready I looked up into the smiling face of my brother, lit by the flames of the fire. He had tears of joy in his eyes; he loved me and I him.

Nikwei and Donald left us together, whispering their goodbyes and laughing as they disappeared into the blackness beneath the dense canopies of the trees. I thanked my brother for giving me the permission I needed to publish and I asked him to explain more to me of what he knew about Tangarua as I needed to hear the unique tribal creation myth again, repeated in its entirety, to enable me to fully understand the spiritual lineage that I had initiated into to reconnect me to my first Grandfather, Tangarua, the great Dragon Lord and the Star Nation from where he came. This time we both connected from the heart, the place of the soul and truth, not from the head, the place of fear, confusion, doubt and ego. Our hearts opened and connected. We were one, the Black and the White Serpents joined together at last in union with our ancient Grandfather, the Black and White Serpent. The Chief fell into a moment of silence, staring into the fire, poking it with a stick sending red sparks flying up into the night sky.

As the Chief lifted his gaze to meet mine, his eyes appeared "vacant" and, as he spoke, it was as if he were being used as a vessel or channel by Spirit, 'Iarueri, Tangarua was from the stars. He came to Tanna Island and mated with Pieria. Pieria had originally come from the stars also but had become human after taking sacred kastom medicine. She was now mortal but was still worshipped as a God (Goddess) by the primitive native peoples. However, because Tangarua and Pieria were not of the same race, their mating and fertilisation initially took place interdimensionally at a higher level of consciousness. In other words, they mated through one or more of their subtle bodies which interpenetrate the physical organism. As they had different genetic and blood lineages (DNA), physical mating that would have been viable at that time would have been impossible.

'The first offspring of this sacred union were twin sons. The firstborn was Majikjiki; the second born Kumesen. Majikjiki had most of the genetic lineage of Tangarua and Kumesen had most of the genetic lineage of Pieria. Majikjiki was born circumcised; Kumesen was not. He had a foreskin. The Christian version of this story is the so-called virgin birth. Now, consider this – if a young woman did not have physical sexual intercourse, she would be officially classed as a virgin, as the skin (hymen) would be unbroken (this is not a foolproof indication, as the hymen can be ruptured naturally through trauma, such as an accident or even strenuous exercise).

'Tangarua was very tall, I mean really tall, and would be classed as a giant. He, like most of the star peoples, were about 12 to 15 feet high, slim with long limbs, fingers and toes. The males had long penises. This is why the tribal peoples of the South Pacific continue to wear the nambas, which is symbolic of the erect phallus to honour and emulate the sacred sexual power of Tangarua and his kind.

'As Majikjiki resembled Tangarua more than his human mother, this also indicated that the star men generally were naturally circumcised. This is the reason why the most important male initiation ceremony, which had crossed the South Pacific to other cultures where the star men had come to earth, was performed. All males wanted to emulate their "Gods" so they could receive their favour, status and power.

'When Majikjiki and Kumesen were born, they crossed the genetic boundary of two unrelated distinct races, which enabled the DNA of the star people to enter the blood lineage of humanity. You could say it was a form of mutation. This is why one of Majikjiki's names, or titles, is "The First One", literally the first hybrid. As Majikjiki was the firstborn of the twins and carried most of his father's blood lineage, he was entrusted to be co-guardian of "The Sacred Waters of Life" along with Tangarua, who brought this elixir with him from his home world (the Chief never mentioned which star system unfortunately). At this time our ancestors lived in a different world than we do now. The lands were vast and there were many species of creatures and beings that are now extinct.

'After some time of living on earth, Tangarua lost his immortality and also became human. He had many other children, all sons. Some did not survive in the early days and were born with physical deformities. Some stories say that Tangarua had 12 sons, others that he had 15 sons. I don't think it really matters. These sons bred with the daughters of the primitive humans, passing the combined genes into a new sub-race, now classified as Australoid (Aust, meaning of the Southern Hemisphere).

'As Tangarua was now mortal, his days were numbered. When he knew he was dying, he gave Pieria and Majikjiki strict instructions on how to dispose of his body at death, which they followed. His body was buried but the skull remained above the ground and covered in volcanic clay. After some time, the crystalline properties of the clay created a chemical reaction with the DNA of the star skull, transforming it into pure crystal. When the clay dried and fell away, the huge crystal skull emerged into the sunshine, drawing to it many magical energies magnetically. Coloured lights shone from within like rainbows. From the left eye socket arose coconut trees and all other fruits. From the right eye socket more of the sacred waters of the star people, the last of the pure elixir. The local people revered the skull for its healing powers and also for its magical abilities to receive and communicate knowledge and therefore wisdom telepathically in any language known to the star races and to those humans who shared their DNA, Majikjiki being one, who was now sole Guardian of the Sacred Pool and, as the firstborn, the next hereditary leader.

'People began to get greedy and power hungry, so an elite priesthood of sorts developed who tried to control access to the sacred skull by force. The skull was a natural offering by Tangarua for the benefit for all of his peoples on earth, not for an elitist group who were fast losing their connection to Spirit. This priesthood soon became corrupted with power and began using the energy of the crystal skull for the wrong reasons. People from different tribes and clans began to fight amongst themselves then wars started. When the hybrid star children died, their skulls became crystalline in nature, depending upon the amount of star DNA in their lineage. These skulls became objects to be revered, worshipped and fought over. Whoever held one of these skulls controlled the masses, probably much like modern religious leaders do today through fear. From these origins, skull worship, then cannibalism spread throughout the lands of the hybrids. People believed that if they ate the flesh of the star hybrids they would also become powerful healers, warriors and chiefs. It soon became a recipe for disaster and butchery ensued, corrupting men for many generations.

'One of the commands that Tangarua gave to Majikjiki before his death was that as sole guardian of "The Sacred Waters of Life" he was not to permit anyone else to go near to the sacred pool. For some reason (which is not clear), Majikjiki allowed Kumesen and his other brothers to bathe in the pool against the will of his father. Pieria, who was working in the fields, heard the boys laughing and splashing in the sacred pool. Horrified, she stormed down to the pool, axe in hand. Kumesen and the others saw her coming and fled into the mountains. She challenged Majikjiki about this, but he lied to his mother. She could see that the pure waters from the star people were, in essence, irreversibly polluted now. The holy waters no longer held the secrets or the connection to the stars. With her axe, she broke down the wild canes which contained the waters, which soaked into the dark volcanic earth, causing the earth to split wide open, where a massive subterranean eruption of water occurred which was so powerful that it began to flood the land. Heavy rain, along with lightning and volcanic activity, rained around them for many days. It became clear that the land that they knew as home was being broken up and destroyed.

'Majikjiki built a great wooden ship (ark) with the help of his hybrid brothers who were compliant in the destruction of their land, along with their wives. Eventually, he gathered all of the known creatures and called the tribe together to come with him, but all refused. Kumesen and his clan remained on Tanna living in the highest mountains. Then three massive tidal waves rose out of the deep, carrying the boat to the West. Kumesen's descendants have been waiting for the descendant of Majikjiki to return ever since that they may be reunited. They would recognise their brothers through the sacred symbol of three.'

The Chief turned away and stared into the fire, indicating he had had enough. I returned.

26th January 2013:
Royal Cloak
I connected again through a shamanic journey with my brother at the nakamal and we sat to talk beneath the clear night sky. Sparks from the fire blew around us; the smoke stung my eyes.

The Chief spoke, the whites of eyes shining in the firelight, 'Iarueri, Majikjiki gave you the royal cloak of feathers some time ago, did he not?'

'Yes, he did,' I replied.

'Describe it to me.'

'Well, the inside of the cloak was made of soft white feathers so, when it was wrapped around your naked body, it felt like velvet or fine silk. The outside of the cloak was made of scarlet and black feathers. The "collar", if you like, was scarlet and the rest of the cloak the deepest black that I had ever seen in feathers.'

'And what significance does this have, do you think?'

I felt a little as though I was being reprimanded but not sure why. I squirmed a little on my log and poked the fire with a stick sending more sparks and smoke into the night sky.

'I don't know what you mean, my brother.'

'Iarueri, when Majikjiki gave you the cloak, he used the word "royal". You initially accepted this statement but, when you rewrote your manuscript for the last book, you removed this title. Why?'

'Brother, I removed it because I felt awkward about that word. I thought this must be my imagination or that my ego was playing tricks with me, trying to trip me up. I didn't want those who read the book to think I thought of myself as superior or special. I am just an ordinary man.'

'That may well be the case but was not the rest of Majikjiki's message valid to your heart? If the rest of his message was true for you, who are you to decide to remove or edit a key word which gives a different meaning on the whole teaching? When Spirit gives you a teaching or insight to be shared with others, they often use key words in their sentences which are energetically active to awaken dormant cellular memory in others through the informational fields of their subtle bodies. If you fall into the ego trap of false humility, denying your true authenticity, you may prevent another soul from fulfilling their destiny at that time. Do not do that again.'

'I am sorry, brother.'

'Majikjiki gave you the royal cloak for a reason. It was his cloak passed down from Tangarua, which he passed on to you. Why are you not using it for your spiritual practices? Majikjiki was the last of the priest kings of Lemuria (see Appendix E) before the great flood. Through this lineage which was granted to you it was your right as the holder of the highest grade in our tribe to receive this mark of authority. The cloak is given because you have earned the right to wear it and the responsibility which it brings. When Majikjiki eventually arrived on your island, he became known by a different name, Manannan. He is known by many names throughout the world, but holds the same energy. His brothers became the rulers of all of the other lands they settled in.'

I had been told off again! The Chief raised his hand and I knew it was time for me to leave.

5th May 2013:
Beltaine

When I was in Itabu, the Chief told me that I had one last ritual to perform which would complete all of my training and initiations. This was to obtain a fish directly from the sea and to cook it on an open fire in my nakamal. The Chief gave me these instructions in October 2012 and yet, even though different fishermen have said that they would definitely get a fish for me, since that time no fish has been forthcoming! I thought this ridiculous, living as we do on an island surrounded by the sea. I was becoming increasingly restless and frustrated by people making me promises and then letting me down. You could suggest that I should go to sea myself and get a fish. As a very poor sailor, the thought of being constantly seasick seriously puts me off. Maybe it was my last test?

The other possibility was that the Chief told me to cook the fish in my nakamal. Well, I didn't have one, so was this the block preventing the fish from materialising, I wondered. For several months now, I have been cleaning up the bottom of the garden and creating a nakamal, building a fire pit for ritual, marking out the four Directions and Elements and having secure fencing erected for privacy. I felt that I had to complete creating the nakamal for the Celtic Fire Festival of Beltaine, so I thought this would be a great opportunity to reconnect physically with the sacred fire of the Itabu nakamal and to mark the exact ninth anniversary of my first initiation of the same Fire Festival in 2003 at Itabu. Maggie was in Dubai visiting family at this time, so I invited some good friends around at sunset to help celebrate this important occasion for me and to create a ceremony to activate the fire pit to connect back to Itabu and the Pacific Rim of Fire.

After my friends had left, I sat at the fire drumming and burning green cupressus branches to create smoke that would smudge and cleanse the nakamal and myself. I also prepared a new staff which I had cut on 22nd December 2012.

2nd June 2013:

Kassoso Stone

The nakamal still did not feel quite right somehow. There was something missing, so I moved the fire pit to a more central location, making sure that I returned the original ash, and repositioned the logs around the perimeter. I suddenly realised that I didn't have a Kassoso stone! I went to the local beach and asked Spirit for the correct stone to be revealed to me, which it was – a sea-tumbled piece of red sandstone about 18 inches high, gathered below the high water mark, which was still covered with sea water and had sand sticking to it. This made a good connection to Majikjiki/Manannan.

I brought the stone home to the nakamal and dowsed for the correct angle so that the stone would be in alignment with Yasur volcano and the Itabu nakamal which was roughly south-east. The Kassoso stone was positioned accordingly, including one of the carvings that was given to me at Itabu. The nakamal was completed at last! All I had to do now was obtain the fish for the final ceremony.

To activate the new ritual site and to honour the Boar, Maggie and I decided to have bacon sandwiches for our supper that evening so the nakamal fire was lit at 5.30 pm. At that very moment, a sparrow hawk flew overhead, which I thought was a good omen. We made offerings of raw bacon (pig) to the fire and to the base of the Kassoso stone, calling to Kassoso to come and feast. Maggie had made a connection with Kassoso on our last visit to Itabu, so I knew she was accepted by them. As Maggie also works with the Mayan medicine wheel, she offered raw chocolate to the fire in this spiritual tradition. I cooked some bacon over the fire, which was burnt on the outside and raw in the centre in true nakamal style!

Maggie went off to bed at nightfall. I remained with the fire until 12.30 am, getting to bed at 1 am. There was no sign of Kassoso.

16th June 2013:

Cooking Fish Ceremony

At 5.45 pm I received an excited call from Helen Young to say that she and her husband Jim were at Peel breakwater (a fishing port in the Isle of Man) where they had obtained a freshly caught mackerel from one of the fishing boats discharging its catch. They were on their way with the fish to me immediately!

I lit the nakamal fire so, by the time Helen and Jim had arrived, it was going nicely. I instinctively knew that this final ceremony had to be completed by the Summer Solstice on 21st/22nd June, when the energy of fire was at its peak.

I had been trained how to kill and butcher sheep on the sheep station in Australia, and had skinned and gutted rabbits in the past, but I had never cleaned and gutted a fish before, so Jim taught me how to do this, then assisted me in impaling the fish on the end of a pointed stick, leaning over the fire to cook in true nakamal style. I followed the Chief's instructions with these preparations.

After the fish was cooked, we placed it on a large leaf "plate" from where I ate it. It tasted delicious. I placed some of the cooked flesh at the base of the Kassoso stone as an offering to Spirit. Jim took several photographs throughout the proceedings, as the Chief had asked for some photos to be taken and sent to him as proof that I had completed this last ceremony. After Helen and Jim had left, I sat by the fire alone, praying to Tangarua, Majikjiki and Kassoso to open a road from Itabu to our nakamal in Manannan's Island.

Cooking the fish ceremony in my nakamal.

In shamanic time, there is no past or future, only the present which is where you place your focus and intent. I recreated the fish ceremony from the beginning, energetically, calling in the spirit of the mackerel. I was amazed as a huge fish manifested that was approximately four feet long by ten inches wide. This creature was magnificent and beautiful. I thanked Spirit for the life of the fish, offering it to the Great Mother (Pieria) Below, the Guardians of the Four Directions and Elements and the Great Father (Tangarua) Above. I removed its head as instructed by the Chief, burying it at the base of a horse chestnut tree at the edge of the nakamal, facing south-east, towards Itabu and Yasur volcano.

By 10.30 pm the light was fading. The evening was still with a patchy clouded sky revealing the moon in her phase of First Quarter. Two bats flew in from the south-east directly above the nakamal, followed shortly afterwards by a hunting barn owl. The owl stayed nearby for about 20 minutes, much to the annoyance of the agitated song birds in their roosts. At 11 pm a solitary bat swooped in from the south-east again to where I sat and circled my head and the nakamal fire before flying off to the north. I thought this was a good omen as Kassoso are represented, not only by fruit bats, but all bats.

I had a sense of inner fulfilment and peace now that the final ceremony had been completed. As I sat by the fire staring into the glowing red embers, I pondered about the link I had made with Kassoso, and would make in the future.

What was its purpose and did it really matter anyway? What does this connection bring to help humanity, if anything?

In my trance-like state I received the following teaching from Spirit.

'When one person achieves something different, such as gaining new knowledge or experience, that energetic signature is automatically activated within the collective human consciousness or, in scientific terms, the Quantum Field. Once this happens, that information raises awareness and therefore brings wisdom about all life on the planet, physical and non-physical, for the benefit of others who wish to make that connection, enabling us all to grow.'

This insight made a lot of sense to me, so I was content with this realisation. I had no further need to keep trying. It was simply just right as it was.

I offered my gratitude to Kassoso for these sacred experiences and for the union of love with Maggie, High Woman Natu Elin.

I left the glowing embers for Kassoso at midnight and went to bed, wrapping my arms around my wife and, in my dreaming state, responding to the call of the great Dragon of Fire and Crystal, to take my place alongside the other Dragon Riders where I rendezvoused with my grandfather, the Great Dragon Lord, Tangarua.

There was work to be done.

Appendices

Appendix A
Cosmic Law

Master M.T. – who lived on the Isle of Man – was (and still is) a member of The White Brotherhood, teaching Cosmic Law. She had three students on the island, one of whom was Maggie. This teaching was a private lesson for her students written in 1993 and is still valid for today giving us a solid foundation on to which we can build our spiritual practices. We have the choice.

Master M.T. passed away in the UK in 2003, entrusting Maggie to burn all of her spiritual teachings written in her private journals. I helped Maggie with this task on the understanding that I would not read any of this material. I honoured the Master's wishes.

Maggie has given permission for this teaching to be published.

The Law

(1) Operate at all times with:
    (a) Immaculate Honesty
    (b) Absolute Integrity
    (c) Total Morality

(2) The correct attitude towards and correct treatment of All Forms of Life

(3) You live with the concept of Peace, Truth, Unconditional Love, Righteousness and Non-Violence.

It is extremely difficult to live by this law – it requires considerable self-discipline.

Comments

Comments are solely for guidance. An individual must interpret as they choose.

In the interpretation is indicated the individual's Karma or evolvement.

Every individual has the right to "choose" – but does not have the right to impose their choice on others.

In the Practice of Law and Order, it is sometimes necessary to curb the choice of the individual for the protection of society.

Comments on Rule 1

(a) **Immaculate Honesty:** in thought, word and deed.

No lies of any shade.

Total Honesty in Financial, Legal, Social and Personal dealings, ie in the way you live your life.

It is sometimes difficult to always know, according to one's evolvement, what comprises Total Honesty.

(b) **Absolute Integrity:** in thought, word and deed. In all your Personal, Business, Social and Financial Dealings.

(c) **Total Morality:** in thought, word and deed.

Comments on Rule 2

The correct attitude towards and correct treatment of *All Forms of Life*.

Human, Animal (including Birds and Fish) – Vegetable, Mineral, Devic, Elemental and The Little People, plus *the Planet*.

ie Everything that dwells within, upon, and around the Earth.

All have a Spark of the Divine, Have Life, Vibrate, Have Feeling and are part of the Created Cosmos.

It is against Cosmic Law to mistreat or abuse any form of life.

Horse racing and dog racing as *practised professionally* by society are abuse – animals will happily join "man" in playing games (unforced activities).

Fishing and shooting for sheer *pleasure* – is abuse. Man should only fish and shoot in his *need* for food.

Comments on Rule 3

You live with the Concept of Peace, Truth, Unconditional Love, Righteousness and Non-Violence.

(a) **Peace:**

The Entire Planet was created for *All Living Creatures to Enjoy.*

Man was not intended to carve up the planet piecemeal to satisfy his Ego, his lust for possession and domination.

Man was intended to live at peace with all forms of life and the planet.

(b) **Truth:**

Means Truth in Speaking, Acting, Assessing – in dealing with *every* aspect of life – Human, Animal, Vegetable, Devic, Elemental and the Little People (those not understood by most people) and Mineral.

It also means – The Truth of Divine Law as laid down by the "Creator of the Universe".

(c) **Unconditional Love:**

This does *not* mean being a doormat and giving in to *all* others, under all circumstances.

It *does* mean dealing with others honestly, fairly, sensibly – with understanding and compassion.

We must say here that genuine criticism is valid, proving it is intended to help and is devoid of malice.

(d)   **Righteousness:** (Right-use-ness)

Right thinking – Right Feeling, Right Speaking, Right Doing.

Basically this means – being at all times *Positive* – in Thinking, Feeling, Speaking and Doing.

You *Think, Feel, Speak or Do* only those things which are *Right, Positive, Good, Helpful* – with regard to *All Life, The Planet* and the *Cosmos.*

You do *not* Think, Feel, Speak or Act – murder, lust, stealing, dishonesty, derogation or disparagement or malice.

(e)   **Non-Violence:**

You do not perpetrate Violence against *any living thing,* ie any *Form of Life – except* – in Self defence or in defence of another – or another form of life.

It is said that the most precious gift, which you can be given, is the gift of life. This gift enables you to "work through" your Karma, ie to return into incarnation as often as it takes to redress any breach of Cosmic Law in previous incarnations, and to further your Evolution.

Thus – if to preserve your life against an aggressor or it is unavoidable that you kill that aggressor – *that*, according to Divine Law, is not murder, either in your own defence or in the defence of another.

It has been given to me that, in this matter of defence of "another form of life" – you do not *unnecessarily* sacrifice your own gift of life – thinking man must use discretion – for a human to give his or her own life, for a mouse, is considered an unnecessary sacrifice. This does not mean that you do not go (perhaps with others) to the defence of Humans or animals who are "en masse" being grossly mistreated merely to satisfy the whim or greed of man.

Finally – for the more advanced Chela (pupil) the following must be added for clarification.

(1)   At this time, in this universe, pain and suffering of the human, animal, vegetable, Devic and mineral Kingdoms – and the Planet – are part of their evolvement.

(2)   "Entities" – there are complete spirits male/female – in the one Entity, created by the "Creator of the Universe" solely to carry out specific tasks – as required by the "Creator" at specific times.

(3)   These "Entities" if incarnate in a physical body (even though they are not subject to Karmic Incarnations) often undergo pain and suffering, in order to take these experiences with them to the next level of consciousness – even to the next Universe, or subsequent Universes.

These experiences, gained through eons of time, are needed for the teaching in, and consequent advancement of, subsequent Universes.

For those who think they can't live up to this law – "upstairs" ask that you should *Try*.

If you know that you have made a mistake – apologise to the "Creator of the Universe" – then continue to *Try*. If you are *genuinely Trying* – lapses should be less frequent.

For example:

If you have recognised, and *correctly dealt with*, this lapse, in this incarnation, you do not carry it over to the next incarnation – to be dealt with, eg Karma (for those who are subject to Karma).

"All religions are but facets of the one Truth and only serve to divide men."

Master M.T.

Appendix B
Soul Cauldrons

The Soul Cauldrons are inspired knowledge given by Caitlin Matthews, my principal teacher in the Celtic shamanic traditions. Over the years of working with this technique it has developed and evolved in its own way. In most traditional shamanic cultures it is understood that the soul has multiple parts. When we experience shock a soul part, or fragment, can detach and remain trapped in the environment of where that trauma took place. These soul parts can be located and returned to the individual through ritual or shamanic intervention.

As I understand it, the ancient Celts believed that we have three principal souls, each of which has a place of "residence" or connection within the three main cavities in our physical bodies, or rather the energetic counterparts. These cavities contain the Soul Cauldrons like a set of interconnecting vessels where each of these souls are nurtured and where the soul consciousness, vitality and memory are stored. These Cauldrons, of course, are not physical but energetic, which means they have the potential to hold immense interdimensional knowledge and wisdom to keep us healthy, enabling us to keep a clear strong connection to Spirit.

The three principal cavities in the body are the belly (Lower Cauldron), the chest (Middle Cauldron) and the head (Upper Cauldron).

The Lower Cauldron is governed by the Vital Soul which is overseen by your Power Animal (such as boar or flying fox)*. This deals with your vitality and power, your connection to the earth, procreation, sex and survival.

Your Middle Cauldron is governed by the Personal Soul which is overseen by the Soul Shepherd, usually a being either animal, human or half and half (such as Kassoso who holds a staff of power)*. This deals with your emotions and passions.

Your Upper Cauldron is governed by your Wisdom Soul such as a Teacher, Angel or Deity (such as Majikjiki)*. This deals with your discernment, clarity, focus and intent and true connection to Spirit.

All of these stacking Cauldrons draw up the vital force of the Earth Mother, from (such as the Dragons of the Molten Seas)*, and draw down into them, rather like a champagne fountain, the vital force of the Sky Father (such as the Dragons of the Seas of Lightning or Tangarua)*. These sacred reservoirs of vital essence fill and drain constantly and can become blocked, stagnant and leak when cracked, broken, dislodged or even turned upside-down.

The three sacred colours representing these Cauldrons, which interestingly are found throughout the indigenous world, are belly – black, heart – red, and head – white (Majikjiki's cloak, for example). If these energetic vessels become blocked through psychic disturbance, or what shamans call "bad" spirits, or through living an unhealthy lifestyle which is stagnant, the vital force flowing between these vessels becomes polluted and energetically "toxic", so sickness develops in the physical organism. By realigning and clearing out these Soul Cauldrons and reconnecting to the governing Soul Aspects we begin to realign our vitality and health.

* The examples relevant to this story.

Caitlin Matthews is acknowledged as a world authority on Celtic wisdom, the Western mysteries and the ancestral traditions of Britain and Europe. She is the author of over 50 books and teaches Celtic Shamanism.

See: www.hallowquest.org.uk

Appendix C
Famadihana

This is a story I wish to share with you. I appreciate that this experience has little in common with the kastom traditions of Itabu but similarly Famidihana is a unique sacred festival in Madagascar which the state and, in particular, the church are trying to stamp out. This is an account of another way of life soon to become extinct through the intolerant, bigoted, prejudiced opinions of those in the West who have influenced and pressurised the local Malagasy people. This section is dedicated to honour the Merina tribal culture and to their ancestors, to whom we are all related.

As a schoolboy I read an article about Famadihana in the National Geographic magazine and was enchanted by the images of people dancing with shroud-wrapped corpses. I was fascinated, even then, with the sacred mysteries between dying and death. There was a memory of sorts, a familiarity of an inner knowing, that persisted to the present day. I knew I simply must experience this ceremony personally.

In 2011 I eventually managed to get a Malagasy contact and email address in Antananarivo, the capital of Madagascar, known locally as Tanna! (Interesting synchronicity, I thought.) After protracted negotiations between my contact and local chiefs who were hosting this festival, I was formally invited to participate by two chiefs in the exhumation ceremonies after providing evidence of my authenticity. It was a huge privilege and I felt really excited about it. Tribal protocol prevents outsiders from attending these sacred ceremonies unless a formal invitation is issued by the host chief, since in Malagasy tribal culture there are very strict rules and taboos, which are known as fady, around dying, death and their sacred tombs in particular.

Maggie and I arrived in Tanna in September of that year and were met by our contact and taken to a pre-booked hotel. The following day I met my driver and guide, who spoke excellent English, and drove me to my first Famadihana ceremony. Maggie had not been officially invited so was not permitted to attend, so she remained in Tanna to do some sightseeing.

As we drove the long distance to Behenjy District my driver explained to me about the festival and some of their tribal culture. We eventually arrived at Tsena'alika where I was formally introduced to Chief Ranaivoandre. Famadihana literally means "the turning of the bones" and is a unique festival where the dead are exhumed, danced with and re-interred back into their family tomb. The festival lasts for three days and three nights.

The first day is preparation, where family members gather after travelling on long arduous journeys from different areas of Madagascar. Dancing, feasting and singing take place as family bring their offerings and gifts, such as zebu (cattle), goats, chickens, fruit, vegetables, rice, alcohol and recently cash. All the money is placed in clean white envelopes which are sealed and the person's name written on the front. This enables the chief to know exactly who provided what and all these offerings are written in the family ledger. Famadihana keeps families together and enables marriages to be arranged, etc.

The last time this particular family's tomb had been opened was 11 years ago in 2000. Most tombs are re-opened about every 7 to 15 years, depending on what the host family can afford.

The second day is also feasting, music and dancing competitions and then the exhumation ceremony.

The third day is more feasting, music, dancing competitions, acrobatics and market stalls where everyone wears their best clothing.

In the past the tribes opened their tombs when they wanted to but now the chiefs have to get official permission from the government and be issued with a certificate of exhumation which has to be displayed to the public. At every tomb opening ceremony a government official, the local mayor and police chief have to be present. Chief Ranaivoandre had invited me to participate in the full three days of Famadihana and offered me a place of honour at his table to share a meal of goat stew and rice.

My driver had instructed me to be ready by 7 am the following morning for an early departure back to Tsena'alika village as the Famidihana ceremony could start at any time during the day, depending when the Panandro (shaman) permitted it in relation to the position of the sun. He also had to tell the chief which path the crowds were to follow to reach the tomb.

By the time the driver and I reached the village; singing and dancing were well under way. Again I was given a place of honour. A scuffle broke out between two drunken men which was soon squashed by others. My guide explained to me what was happening since this was the most important day.

People suddenly stopped, looking towards the chief as he approached. Word had been given by the Panandro to go now! Everyone moved like a gathering swarm of locusts across the fields and scrub to the white square tomb built on top of a distant hill where we all gathered. A brass band played music on the roof of the tomb as others set up food and drink stalls. All carried newly woven mats to be wrapped around the corpses. Speeches were made and the certificate of exhumation displayed. Everyone fell silent as the Panandro stood silently facing the entrance of the tomb, his back to the sun, his arms reaching out to feel the energy or perhaps the spirits of the ancestors drawing close. The Panandro gave the signal to the chief who instructed the tomb to be opened. How exciting!

Chief Ranaivoandre told me to stand before the tomb at the front of the crowd. I was permitted to take photographs. The cement seals around the granite stone slabs that had sealed the tomb for 11 years were broken by two men with hammers. The crowd was in a frenzy; the atmosphere was electric and charged with emotion as people cried, wailed and laughed. They were about to hold their loved ones in their arms again after so long. People surged forward and were told to move back.

The granite slabs were manhandled to either side of the tomb opening, revealing a deep blackness within. I was told by my guide to wait a few minutes to allow the bad air to escape, then several men went into the tomb carrying lighted candles, disappearing into the darkness. The Chief told me to go inside the tomb. It wasn't a request; it was a command. I ventured into the cool musty blackness, descending into the tomb via a steep slope. When my eyes had adjusted to the flickering candlelight I saw that the tomb was lined with granite slabs and, at different levels, were recesses upon which were laid countless wrapped corpses on mats. At the highest level in the tomb was a separate recess reserved for the chiefs and this was decorated with sacred symbols and patterns of large coloured diamond shapes around this inner entrance.

The oldest corpse came out head first and, as soon as he emerged into the sunlight, a cry went up in the crowd and they became frenzied, wanting their bodies out next. Each corpse was carried out in strict order of rank or ancestral age. Some of the shrouds were a rusty red colour or black with mould when they first emerged from the tomb. As soon as the bodies were brought out into the sunshine the families danced with the corpses, holding them above their heads as they laughed and cried. Some people sat with their corpses across their laps as they ate and drank, offering food and drink to their deceased. Some people were drunk with local alcohol, offering this to their dead.

The corpses of the children were held high above the heads of their fathers as they danced with them, calling out their names, touching their hearts gently with their calloused hands. Tears ran down their faces. Some sat in silence, offering prayers to their dead, gently stroking their wrapped bodies with their hands and kissing their shrouded heads. New mats were wrapped around them and the families rewrapped the bodies in white sheets and retied them tightly with ropes. Their names were rewritten on the shrouds with felt tip pen.

The Chief came up to me and told me through my interpreter that when he dies he also will be put in this tomb and his family will dance and feast with him. He was crying with joy at the thought of this family reunion.

The old stained mats that the corpses were laid upon in the tomb were brought out and were rolled up so the family could take them back home with them as souvenirs. My guide explained that these mats will be placed in the north-east corner of their house, which is the place reserved for their ancestors. Nobody is permitted to sit there with the only exception of the monarch who is seen as the intermediary between humans and the spirit world (Madagascar used to be divided up into several kingdoms pre-colonial oppression). If a royal tomb was opened, the bones were taken to the river to be washed then re-interred. Each district still retains the lineage of the royal bloodline, which is no longer recognised by the colonial-backed state. My guide explained that the king is not permitted to die in their culture so, when he is close to death, he is killed with a special spear through the heart. The king's clavicles (collarbones) are then cut out with a ritual knife and placed in a jar, his organs disposed of in the river. This ritual is to prevent the royal lineage and power from being lost, which they believe it would be if the king died naturally. The remains of the king's body are then laid in the tomb. The royal clavicles represent the king's continued support for his community after his death. The local name for the king is Apanjaka and only the king is permitted to wear red, especially during ceremony.

My guide also explained it was fady to have the grandmother's ancestral lineage laying alongside the grandfather's ancestral lineage, so these had separate tombs on different sides of the valley.

The Panandro gave the word to put the bodies back. He was looking at the sun. The corpses had to be returned and the tomb sealed before the sun set. As the tomb entrance faced due west, this allowed the last rays of the sun to bathe the doorway. New mats were placed inside the tomb and the bodies returned, newly wrapped and renamed, in strict sequence. Everyone was silent except for gentle sobbing. As the men resealed the large granite slabs across the tomb entrance with cement, the Panandro stood with his back to the sun incanting prayers as the tomb was resealed for the next few years.

If somebody in the family dies between openings they are buried in a grave at the side of the tomb, then their body is put in the tomb at the next Famadihana festival. In some areas of the country, if a body is put into a coffin, the coffin is packed with sweet potato leaves then the coffin is sealed and plastered in thick zebu manure to keep it airtight.

We returned to Tanna. I returned to Tsena'alika village the following day for the final day of feasting, dancing, competitions, acrobatics and stalls. On the second Famidihana, I asked my guide for permission for Maggie to attend with me, which thankfully was granted.

We set off to travel to Ambatolampy District to meet Chief Razafimamonjisoa at Ambatomenaloha village. The last time the main tomb was opened here was nine years ago. The four-wheel drive journey was adventurous to say the least and, on our arrival at the village, we were greeted by the Chief who invited us to share a meal of zebu meat and rice with him and his family in his house. Maggie gave the Chief's wife a crystal bracelet.

Two tombs were being opened today but, for some reason, the Panandro delayed the exhumation which caused the crowd to become very anxious and agitated. Eventually the word came through and we joined the swarm of people moving en masse across the fields and up and down steep hills to the tombs. We couldn't get near to the tombs because of the jostling crowds but at least Maggie saw the corpses coming out of the tombs and being danced with. Our guide explained that the Roman Catholic church permitted Famadihana (very gracious) but that the Protestants were trying their hardest to stamp it out, causing serious family rifts as some local people turned against their ancient customs.

We returned for the following day to watch the slaughtering of many zebu, pigs and goats before the festivities. I was deeply touched by the generosity and kindness of the local people; many were very poor, living a subsistence lifestyle, sharing all they had with us. I prayed to the Great Mother that they may retain the sacred links with their ancestors and that, in time, they would join their loved ones in the family tombs, so that they too may be honoured.

Appendix D
Tribal Tattoos (Natadao)

The following two illustrations are of my tribal Grade Marks. They have been sketched freehand so are not symmetrical. They are not meant to be perfect pieces of art work.

In a tribal culture the tattoo is drawn freehand, then the design created by rhythmically puncturing the skin with needles or, traditionally, citrus thorns, until the wound bleeds. A mixture of charcoal, lamp soot, coconut oil and kastom plant juices is rubbed into the raw flesh, then the procedure repeated. After the tattoo has been completed, a thick paste of the tattoo mixture is applied over the wound and left in place for about three days and nights without washing.

It is a very painful process which changes the informational fields of the body.

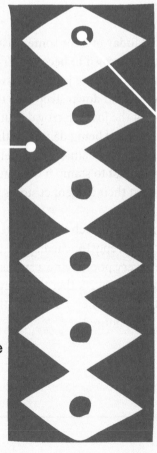

Kassoso

Grade Mark of a newly established High Chief

Represents different Spirit Stories

Date received:
27th October 2005
Tattooist:
Isul
Position:
Upper right arm, to face enemy in battle, displaying your lineage and rank (established hereditary High Chief – indentations are smaller and more numerous).

Represents different initiations such as Hereditary Lineage, Cannibalism, Opening Skulls, Warrior/Tribal Warfare, Hunting and Circumcision

Each time a Grade Mark is given it is slightly different depending upon the muscle mass and tone of the body and the tribal lineage of the tattooist.

A tribal tattoo which is a Grade Mark cannot be given unless it has been earned. In a culture that could not read or write, your tribal body marks indicated your blood lineage and grade. The tattoo impregnates the energy body so connects the receiver of this mark to the tribal spiritual lineage and the Guardian Consciousness / Deity / Archetype who oversees that lineage.

If you have not prepared yourself through ritual, ceremony, tests and trials to bear this mark and the energy you are now aligned to, you can get seriously sick and possibly die.

Warning: Do not copy these tattoos unless you have earned the right to be aligned with this specific lineage.

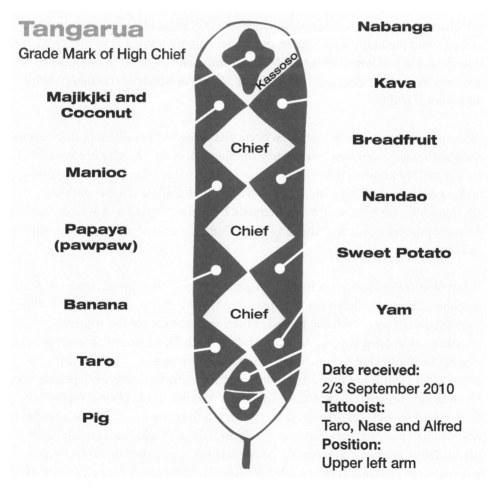

Tangarua
Grade Mark of High Chief

Majikjki and
Coconut

Manioc

Papaya
(pawpaw)

Banana

Taro

Pig

Kassoso

Chief

Chief

Chief

Nabanga

Kava

Breadfruit

Nandao

Sweet Potato

Yam

Date received:
2/3 September 2010
Tattooist:
Taro, Nase and Alfred
Position:
Upper left arm

Appendix E
Lemuria

I do not know why the Chief used the word Lemuria, as I had always understood Lemuria to be the lost continent in the Indian Ocean between Madagascar and Indonesia. It had been suggested by occultists that the lost continent of Lemuria gave its name to the lemur, an arboreal primate of several species unique to Madagascar and adjacent islands.

From my research I have generally found that the lost continent of multiple islands in the Pacific Ocean was known as Mu, but both names seem to be interchangeable, which is confusing. The lost continent in the Atlantic Ocean, of course, was Atlantis and, interestingly, one of Manannan's titles was "God of Atlantis". As the Chief used the name Lemuria I will keep to this but, to be clear, I am talking about the lost continent in the Pacific Ocean.

Scientists have found no physical evidence of any of these lost continents that they care to admit publicly but, of course, most scientists are trained to be blinkered and restrictive and will not consider the bigger picture with all of the possibilities of land masses in other dimensions or parallel existences which interpenetrate third dimensional reality.

From my research I have learned that occultists recognise 144 different dimensions, along with many overtones associated with them, all of which carry life forms. If there are 144 known dimensions and we are in the third then, in essence, this makes humanity nothing more than "pond life" in the whole scheme of things, yet, thankfully, we hold within our energetic DNA the awareness to awaken the dormant possibilities of reconnecting to the Great Cosmic Mother, our true origins and lineage.

When multiple indigenous cultures have similar myths, then the ancestors were probably accessing collective consciousness in other dimensions where the Beings there interacted with the tribal medicine men and women and the authentic priesthood in ancient temples and sacred sites which "downloaded" knowledge and wisdom for the benefit of humanity. Myth is based upon fact which is usually an oral tradition and is not permitted to be changed in any way, whereas legend is open for embellishment and exaggeration by each storyteller. These ancient myths have been passed down from generation to generation from the first telling by somebody who had had personal experience in the Pacific Islands, including Hawaii, Easter Island, Tahiti, Samoa and Aotearoa (New Zealand), where the Maoris called this lost continent Hawaiki. Some people have been hypnotically regressed to experience past lives as citizens in Mu, Lemuria and Atlantis. Is this their dormant cellular memory awakening?

Lemuria was said to be principally a feminine oriented race, whereas Atlantis was said to be principally a masculine oriented race. It is said that the star people lost their immortality when they came to earth, dying as mortal humans. However, according to myth, a married couple in Lemuria regained their immortality through sacred tantra; they were known as Ay and Tiya (Ay was the male and Tiya the female). Ay and Tiya taught this practice to initiates creating a mystery school called the Naakal or Naacal (is this where the name nakamal came from?). These initiates became known as the Naakals. The Naakals knew that Lemuria was going to be destroyed so 1,000 of them left and went to the newly emerging continent of Atlantis. From Atlantis they went to other powerful sacred areas of the world to set up more mystery schools, including Egypt where, interestingly, a bust of Tiya still survives.

Appendix F
High Chief Wai Wai Rawi's Family Tree

Traditionally the tribal lineage holders would remember every High Chief back to the first Grandfather – rather like the Druidic Bards of our lineage. When the Christian missionaries came they knew that by systematically executing the lineage holders the tribe would become disconnected and therefore leaderless and weak. Had that *not* occurred, we would have had a long lineage back into antiquity. As it is Rawi is the furthest back that the Chief can go in living memory.

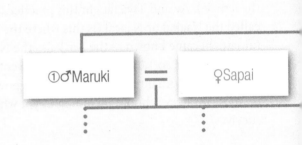

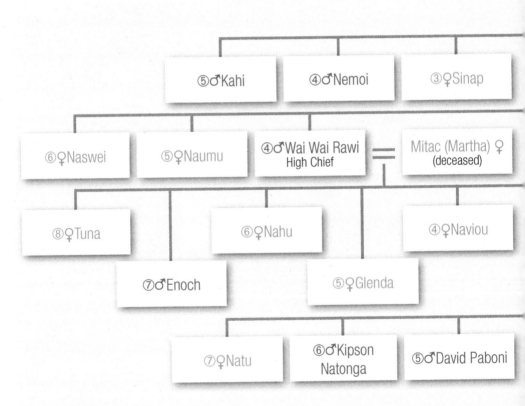

♀ = female
♂ = male

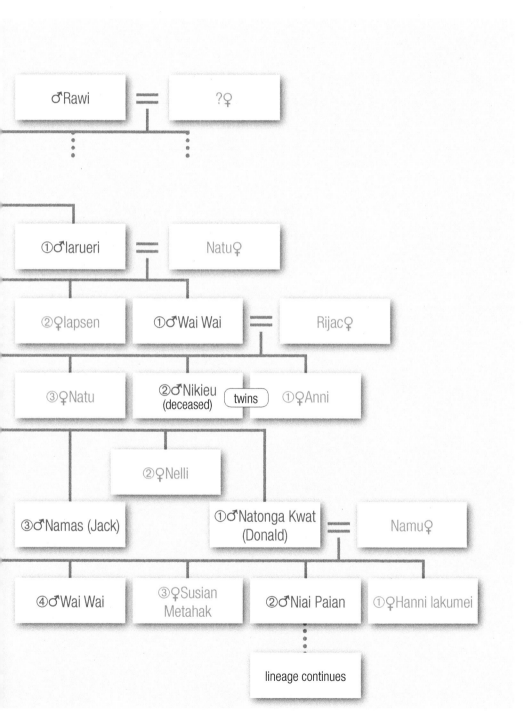

Kassoso

9 780953 331666